Table of Contents

Introduction..1

Terminology.. 2

History of Cannabis.................................... 4

Cannabis Anatomy.................................... 7

General Concepts 10

Alternatives to Organics 11

Synthetic vs Organic Fertilizers 14

Removing soil Contaminates 16

Organic Pesticides.. 18

Herbicides: 19

Organic Fungicides... 21

Diseases and Insect Pests 25

Principles of Plant Protection 26

Fungal Diseases... 28

Gray Mold (Botrytis) 29

Fusarium 31

Verticilium... 32

Bacterial Diseases 33

Viruses... 34

Insect Pests 35

Aphids and Ants 36

Red Spider Mites 37

Fungus Gnats 38

Whiteflies 39

Thrips 40

Caterpillars 41

Snails and slugs 42

Leaf miners 43

Borers 44

Nematodes 46

Nutrients: Deficiencies and Excesses 47

Organic Insecticides 49

Biological Control. 54

Indicator Plants 55

Mycorrhiza 57

Tensiometers 61

Relative Humidity 62

CO2 63

Growing Medicinal Cannabis 64

Growing Mother Plants 66

Preparation of Clones 68

Lighting 71

Light Intensity 73

Abundant Light: 74

LEDs 75

Electricity in the Greenhouse 78

Fertilizer Requirements 79

Micronutrients 80

Organic Fertilizers 83

Renewal of Plants 89

Growth Media 90

Growing Methods 92

Traditional Organic Production 93

Weekly Checklist 97

Calculating the CFM for your Greenhouse 100

Growing in vessels with artificial media 101

Hydroponics 102

Nutrient Film Technique 109

Aeroponics 112

References 115

PRODUCTION OF MEDICINAL CANNABIS IN GREENHOUSES

Barry Nadel

ISBN: 9798215855447

Introduction

Welcome to the world of Cannabis growing. This guide will provide you with all the information you need to grow and maintain your cannabis plants in your Agro4pro Mini Professional Greenhouse.

The information provided in this manual is based on peer-reviewed scientific articles published in reputable journals.

Like all plants, Cannabis needs a few minutes of attention each day. The manual provides you with short summations of important background information, which will allow you to react quickly and correctly to all your growing challenges.

Growing Cannabis does not differ from growing any other crop. There is no magic, voodoo or mystical components to growing this crop. A positive attitude is beneficial to all living things and research has proven this concept.

Successful agricultural ventures aren't simple. There are many factors, environmental, nutritional, growing media, light, water and pest control that go into a successful or disastrous growing season. However, the better prepared you are, the more likely the chance you will be successful in growing cannabis.

The design of the manual provides first background information to better understand how to grow your crop.

Terminology

Figure 1. Cannabis Flowers.

There is confusion concerning terminology, especially since different governments define Cannabis differently.

Cannabis, hemp, marijuana, pot, Maryjane, weed, etc. are terms for the same genera. Interspecies crossing refute the Botanists that separate the Cannabis genus into three different species. The three accepted species, Sativa, Indica and Ruderalis cross easily and produce fertile offspring. The accepted biological definition of a species is: organisms are within the same species if they can interbreed to produce viable, fertile offspring.

Prezygotic and postzygotic barriers separate species from one another. These barriers prevent mating or the production of viable, fertile offspring. The accepted botanical divisions need revision.

Medical Cannabis is the same as recreational cannabis but used for different purposes.

Hemp is the name of the fiber from the stock of the Cannabis plant. They have bred hemp varieties for fiber production and not flower production. Because of international regulations hemp varieties can't have over 0.3% of the cannabinoid Tetrahydrocannabinol (THC the primary psychoactive chemical). However, several governments define any Cannabis variety with less than 0.3% THC as hemp, even though the variety isn't for fiber production.

We define cannabinoids as a group of assorted chemical compounds[1] which interact with cannabinoid receptors[2]. Cannabinoid receptors (CB1 and CB2) are part of the natural human endocannabinoid system in cells that alter neurotransmitters release[3]d in the brain[4].

Cannabidiol (CBD) is the second most important cannabinoid. CBD is not a psychoactive compound. There are over 110 different cannabinoids isolated from cannabis, which cause a variety of physiological effects.

Terpenes are the chemicals responsible for the flavors and odors of cannabis. Researchers have identified a hundred and fifty terpenes in Cannabis resin. Terpinoids are a modified class of terpenes with varying functional groups, and the oxidized methyl group moved or removed at various positions. They divide terpenes into monoterpenes, sesquiterpenes, diterpenes, sesterpenes, and triterpenes, depending on its carbon units. Terpenes and terpenoids are both hydrocarbons. Terpenoids are denatured terpenes by oxidation (drying and curing the flowers). The industry uses the words terpenes and terpenoids interchangeably, but as pointed out above, they are different.

Clones (or rooted cuttings) are asexually reproduced plants for a mother plant, making them genetically identical.

Autoflowering is a trait that makes the plant insensitive to daylength. The plant no longer needs 12-hour days to flower.

Feminized plants come from seeds bred to produce only female plants. This is done by inducing a female plant to produce male flowers. The pollen used is still genetically female. So, the seed produced will be over 90% female.

---

1. https://en.wikipedia.org/wiki/Chemical_compound

2. https://en.wikipedia.org/wiki/Cannabinoid_receptor

3. https://en.wikipedia.org/wiki/Neurotransmitter_release

4. https://en.wikipedia.org/wiki/Brain

History of Cannabis

The written history of cannabis dates back to at least five thousand years. The Chinese used cannabis for medicine and a means of reaching a euphoric state of mind since antiquity. Archaeological evidence indicates its use well before then. Many historical accounts describe it had valued the plant for fiber to make strong rope, as food and medicine. Cannabis's psychoactive properties found uses in religious and recreational use.

The indigenous source of Cannabis is Central Asia and the Indian subcontinent. Chinese Emperor Shen Nung, known as the Father of Chinese Medicine, wrote concerning Cannabis's use in treating rheumatism, gout, malaria, and absent-mindedness[1].

Cannabis spread from China to Korea[2], India and to Eastern Africa[3]. The Indians celebrated Cannabis in one of the Sanskrit Vedic hymns. They called it an herb that releases us from anxiety[4]. Ancient doctors prescribed Cannabis for pain relief and cautioned against excess use.

An Egyptian papyrus[5] from 1500 B.C. mentions cannabis as a useful way to treat inflammation.

In the Arab world, references to hashish began to show up between 800 A.D.[6] and 1000 A.D. The plant's intoxicating effects[7] became emphasized around this time. Muslims used marijuana for recreational use since the Koran banned

1. https://www.medicaldaily.com/brief-history-medical-cannabis-ancient-anesthesia-modern-dispensary-370344

2. https://www.livescience.com/48337-marijuana-history-how-cannabis-travelled-world.html

3. http://content.time.com/time/health/article/0,8599,1931247,00.html

4. https://www.livescience.com/48337-marijuana-history-how-cannabis-travelled-world.html

5. https://www.medicaldaily.com/brief-history-medical-cannabis-ancient-anesthesia-modern-dispensary-370344

6. https://www.history.com/topics/crime/history-of-marijuana

7. https://www.hellomd.com/health-wellness/5ad6746f049b4f000a64e890/marijuanas-storied-history-from-ancient-times-to-now

alcohol consumption, but marijuana was not. Hindus in India revered the use of marijuana in a mildly intoxicating drink called bhang, saying that it cured a long list of ills[8], including problems with sunstroke, digestion and dysentery.

During the sixteenth century, the Spanish brought cannabis to the New World to produce hemp fiber. Hemp became an important product as the European countries expanded their rule over the four corners of the earth. They made canvas for sails and nautical ropes from hemp. Over 120,000 pounds, of hemp[9] ropes were needed to make the rigging for the original U.S.S. Constitution.

---

8. https://books.google.com/
books?id=pGgzBgAAQBAJ&pg=PA21&lpg=PA21&dq=It+cures+dysentery+and+sunstroke,+clears+p
hlegm,+quickens+digestion,+sharpens+appetite,+makes+the+tongue+of+the+lisper+plain,+freshens+th
e+intellect+and+gives+alertness+to+the+body+and+gaiety+to+the+mind.+Such+are+the+useful+and
+needful+ends+for+which+in+His+goodness+the+Almighty+made+bhang.&source=bl&ots=V3706R
GJzJ&sig=wYPjhH6PWwvJ9iClny5L3E9FWPQ&hl=en&sa=X&ved=0ahUKEwi1j6DL1LnKAhWCW
SYKHfmgA6wQ6AEIIDAA#v_43ec3e5dee6e706af7766ffffea512721_onepage_6cff047854f19ac2aa52aa
c51bf3af4a_q_43ec3e5dee6e706af7766ffffea512721_It_0bcef9c45bd8a48eda1b26eb0c61c869_20cures_0
bcef9c45bd8a48eda1b26eb0c61c869_20dysentery_0bcef9c45bd8a48eda1b26eb0c61c869_20and_0bcef9c
45bd8a48eda1b26eb0c61c869_20sunstroke_0bcef9c45bd8a48eda1b26eb0c61c869_2C_0bcef9c45bd8a4
8eda1b26eb0c61c869_20clears_0bcef9c45bd8a48eda1b26eb0c61c869_20phlegm_0bcef9c45bd8a48eda1
b26eb0c61c869_2C_0bcef9c45bd8a48eda1b26eb0c61c869_20quickens_0bcef9c45bd8a48eda1b26eb0c6
1c869_20digestion_0bcef9c45bd8a48eda1b26eb0c61c869_2C_0bcef9c45bd8a48eda1b26eb0c61c869_2
0sharpens_0bcef9c45bd8a48eda1b26eb0c61c869_20appetite_0bcef9c45bd8a48eda1b26eb0c61c869_2C
_0bcef9c45bd8a48eda1b26eb0c61c869_20makes_0bcef9c45bd8a48eda1b26eb0c61c869_20the_0bcef9c4
5bd8a48eda1b26eb0c61c869_20tongue_0bcef9c45bd8a48eda1b26eb0c61c869_20of_0bcef9c45bd8a48e
da1b26eb0c61c869_20the_0bcef9c45bd8a48eda1b26eb0c61c869_20lisper_0bcef9c45bd8a48eda1b26eb0
c61c869_20plain_0bcef9c45bd8a48eda1b26eb0c61c869_2C_0bcef9c45bd8a48eda1b26eb0c61c869_20fr
eshens_0bcef9c45bd8a48eda1b26eb0c61c869_20the_0bcef9c45bd8a48eda1b26eb0c61c869_20intellect_
0bcef9c45bd8a48eda1b26eb0c61c869_20and_0bcef9c45bd8a48eda1b26eb0c61c869_20gives_0bcef9c45
bd8a48eda1b26eb0c61c869_20alertness_0bcef9c45bd8a48eda1b26eb0c61c869_20to_0bcef9c45bd8a48e
da1b26eb0c61c869_20the_0bcef9c45bd8a48eda1b26eb0c61c869_20body_0bcef9c45bd8a48eda1b26eb0
c61c869_

9. https://www.farmcollector.com/farm-life/strategic-fibers

In 1925, an international conference took place in The Hague[10]. The title of the conference was the International Opium Convention[11]. The conference banned exportation of "Indian hemp" to countries that had prohibited its use. It required importing countries to issue certificates of importation and stating that the shipment is "exclusively for medical or scientific purposes". The participants signed on a treaty that required them to "exercise an effective control of such a nature as to prevent the illicit international traffic in Indian hemp and especially in the resin". The US Congress passed the Marihuana Tax Act[12] in 1937. This law prohibited the production of hemp along with cannabis.

---

10. https://en.wikipedia.org/wiki/The_Hague

11. https://en.wikipedia.org/wiki/International_Opium_Convention

12. https://en.wikipedia.org/wiki/Marihuana_Tax_Act_of_1937

Cannabis Anatomy

As mentioned before, botanist still divide cannabis into three species. Figure 2 below outlines their general anatomical differences between the species.

Figure 2. Cannabis plant morphology

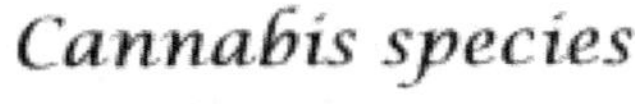

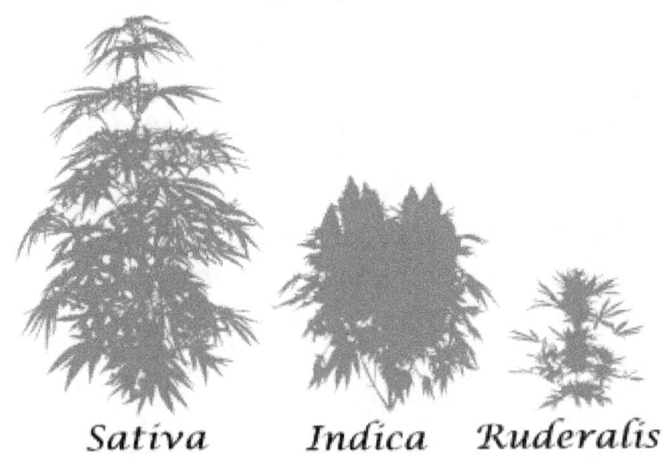

The three cannabis species have different leaves shapes. Figure3 demonstrates the variation in leaf morphology.

The female cannabis flower is the source of the chemically rich oils so highly sought after. Figure 4 below shows the female cannabis flower's unique morphology.

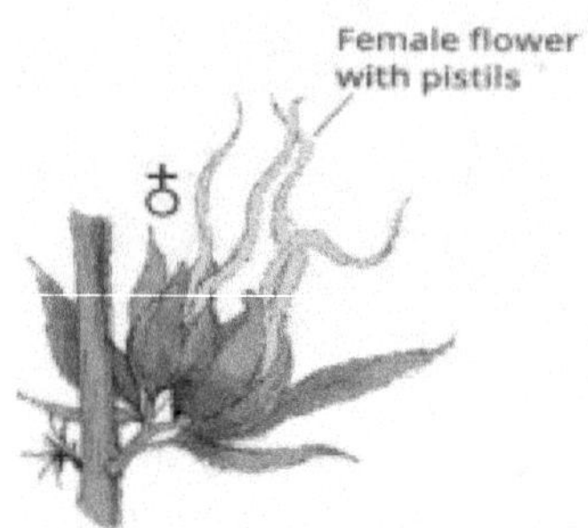

Figure 4. Female Cannabis Flower

Male flowers are disastrous for your yield. If pollinated, female flowers they produce seed and little oil.

They have documented feminized Cannabis plants many times to produce male flowers. Figure 5 shows the structure of the male flower.

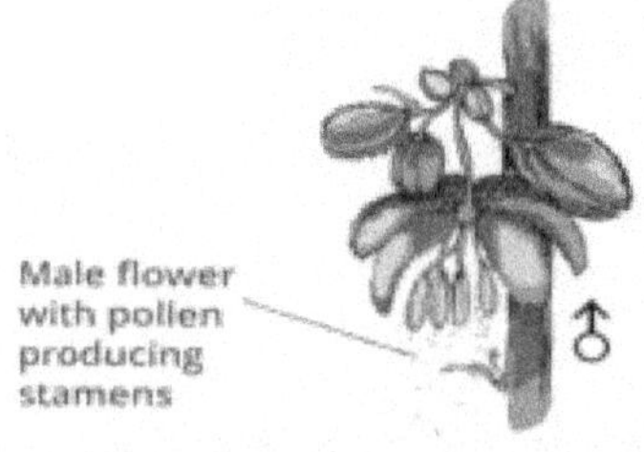

Figure 5. Male Cannabis flower.

Don't let the male reach maturity and release pollen. Cannabis is wind pollinated. Any air movement will carry the pollen away to pollinate female plants. The best method of removing male flowers is to cover them with a bag to contain any pollen dispersion and then cut the stem off the plant. Keep the mouth of the bag closed, remove it to outside the greenhouse.

Maintain good root health is critical to good growth. Figure 6 below is a cross section of a Cannabis root.

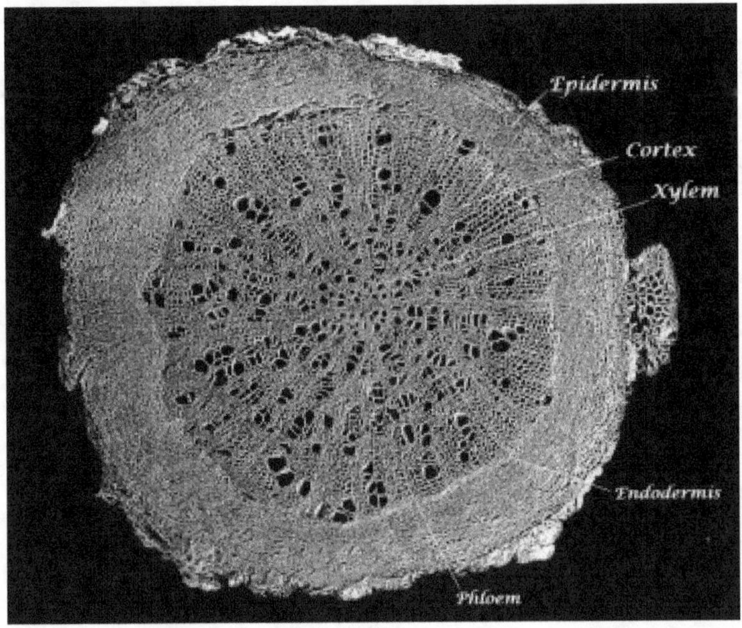

Figure 6. Cross section of a cannabis root.

Roots are also used for medicinal reasons to treat joint pain, inflammation, fever, skin burns, and cessation of hemorrhage after childbirth. Boiled roots extracts were also used to reduce infants' vomiting.

Hydroponically grown Cannabis has clean roots easy to harvest.

General Concepts

Agro4pro designed the Mini Professional Greenhouse (MPG) to grow crops throughout the entire year in harsh environments. The greenhouse is a platform to grow any crop. Our growing manuals are available to help the grower be more successful.

This manual will help you grow cannabis from its initial stages until harvest. The processes of drying, curing and extraction aren't actions taken in the greenhouse, and aren't covered in this manual.

Alternatives to Organics

This manual is proposing an alternative to organic (ATO) growing of Cannabis for two reasons. First, to make it safer for human consumption. Second to facilitate a system of growth that will allow repeatable results of the Cannabis chemical profile. They define organic crops as food[1] produced by methods that observe with the principles of organic farming[2]. The regulations vary worldwide. Organic farming strives to cycle resources, promote ecological balance, restrict synthetic pesticides, and reserve biodiversity[3]. Most organizations regulating organic products restrict certain pesticides[4] and fertilizers[5] in farming. Many countries require a connection between soil and the plant to call it organic production. The vast majority of organic foods aren't processed using irradiation[6], industrial solvents or synthetic food additives[7].

This alternative concept answers several problems that organic growing doesn't deal. Most people believe organic crops are safer to eat than non-organic crops. However, regulations for organic growing miss several important safety features. They are:

Organic regulations don't require testing the water used in irrigation for pollutants such as pesticides, fertilizers, and heavy metals.

Don't require testing of the soil for pollutants such as pesticides, fertilizers, and heavy metals.

Don't require treating the runoff water for excess fertilizer, pesticides, or other harmful products.

---

1. https://en.wikipedia.org/wiki/Food

2. https://en.wikipedia.org/wiki/Organic_farming

3. https://en.wikipedia.org/wiki/Biodiversity

4. https://en.wikipedia.org/wiki/Pesticide

5. https://en.wikipedia.org/wiki/Fertilizer

6. https://en.wikipedia.org/wiki/Irradiation

7. https://en.wikipedia.org/wiki/Food_additives

This alternative concept is to make sure you grow unpolluted crops by testing both the soil and water for contaminates. Why consume organically grown crops produced on polluted soil or irrigated with contaminated water?

A crop grown under this alternative method manner.

1. Organic doesn't allow the use of artificial

media. ATO encourages the use of sterile

artificial media to produce cleaner crops.

1. Organic is concerned with the use of

pesticides and other poisons.

1. ATO emphasizes ecologically safe

pesticides, and demands careful use of

pesticides, including protecting the sprayer (with

proper protective gear) and maintaining the

proper interval of time from employing the

pesticide before consumption.

4. ATO considers the overall quality of the

agricultural water for human consumption,

not only pesticides, but heavy metals, sewage,

and poisons from any source.

1. ATO crops will be grown in sterile artificial

media free of sewage, poisons and free of heavy

metal toxicity.

1. Organic fertilizers are great for recreational cannabis. However, medical cannabis demands repeatability. The nutrient regime affects the levels of cannabinoids and terpenes. You need exact control on your fertilization to repeat the same chemical profile season after season.

Synthetic vs Organic Fertilizers

In popular literature and especially on the internet, articles are published without peer evaluation. This causes many misconceptions to circulate in the public. However, if you read the scientific papers on the subjects, you find that the fundamental problem with modern agriculture isn't the technologies, but human abuse.

The problem with synthetic fertilizers they break down slower in nature and overused by farmers. The various components of the fertilizer leak into the ground water and from there spread throughout the ecosystem.

Another area of misconception is Genetically Modified Organisms (GMOs). There is no significant scientific research to substantiate the "evils of Genetically Modified Organisms". There are no reports of GMO foods causing damage to humans or animals. What happens often is the misuse of herbicides. Many of the GMO crops have resistance to the herbicide Roundup. Unfortunately, many farmers over spray, keeping their fields clean of weeds and thus increasing their yields. However, this abuse of herbicide leaves trace amounts in the food and pollutes ground water.

Toxicological research found the following results: "These results demonstrate that dsRNA for insect control does not produce adverse health effects in mammals at oral doses millions to billions of times higher than anticipated human exposures and so poses a negligible risk to mammals (Petrick, et al. 2016).

People opposed to GMOs speak of the evils they create as if they will slowly kill you. The actual problems lie with the farmer's excessive use of pesticides and fertilizers. It would be political suicide to attack farmers. There is a simple solution: Test crops for pesticide residues. If a farmer's crop shows higher levels of pesticides than permitted by health authorities, then destroy the crop.

There is no better way to control misuse than to hit the offender in the pocketbook. The fear of losing one's livelihood will stop the abuse. We should analyze crops for pesticides. The public will also have a better idea of what they are eating.

The same situation exists with synthetic fertilizer. Once again, the fundamental problem is overuse. Many farmers "pump" their crops with nitrogen to increase size so they will get better prices. The solution is not to outlaw the fertilizer, but to regulate its use.

ATO proposes greenhouses treat their runoff water before it returns into the ecosystem. Treatment ponds need with aquatic plants are efficient at removing nitrogen, phosphates, and potassium from the water. Test the water and release it back into the ecosystem until approval by health authorities.

Removing soil Contaminates

The old method of removing soil contaminates was to physically remove the contaminated soil. Mushrooms, bacteria and growing plants can help contain or reduce heavy metal pollution. This is called phytoremediation (EPA, 1988). It has the advantage of relatively low cost and wide public acceptance (Schnoor, 1997). Trees and grass are planted around the contaminated area to reduce erosion and the spread of the contamination. This method confines the pollutant and reduces its spread to non-contaminated soils.

Phytoextraction is a method of growing plants on contaminated soils that can remove heavy metals from soils by absorbing them into their tissues. At the end of the growing season harvest, dry and burn the crop in a place that would re-infect the soil. The heavy metals can be found in the ash. Recovery rate of pollutant is depended on the quantity of pollutants in the ground. Recovery rates are from grams to kilos/$1000m^2$.

Rhizofiltration is another method of removing heavy metal contamination. In this method roots extract heavy metals. In an experiment employing sunflower on floating rafts, it removed radioactive metals from water in ponds at Chernobyl (EPA 2000) and cleaned up a uranium plant in Ohio.

Brazil has several abandoned gold mines leaking mercury and other heavy metals into the soil and water. Mercury is one of the most toxic of heavy metals and is readily past along in the food chain. Grass growing on contaminated soil and eaten by cows pass the mercury onto us. Brazilian farmers now grow maize and canola in those areas. Both species absorb gold and mercury. Up to a kilogram/ hectare of gold has been extracted from the plants after harvest.

Experiments with mustard greens removed 45% of the excess lead from a yard in Boston, to improve the safety of children who play there. In Trenton, New Jersey, they employed pumpkin vines to clean up an old factory. The British used Alpine pennycress to help clean up abandoned mines.

Yellow poplars can convert a toxic form of mercury to a more benign form.

Water ferns, blue sheep fescue and members of the cabbage family absorb lead from polluted water sources and soil. Smooth water hyssop takes up copper and mercury out of bodies of water. One superstar is water hyacinths. They absorb mercury, lead, cadmium, zinc, cesium, strontium-90, uranium and various pesticides. Sunflowers can also remove a wide range of compounds for example; uranium and strontium-90 from radioactive sites. They can also remove cesium, methyl bromide, zinc and copper from the soil. Bladder campion accumulates zinc and copper, while Indian mustard greens concentrate selenium, Sulphur, lead, chromium, cadmium, nickel, zinc, and copper.

Perhaps the most magnificent hyper-accumulator is the willow tree, Salix viminalis. Willow absorbs copper, zinc, cadmium, selenium, silver, chromium, uranium, petrochemicals and many others. Once its bio-mass has concentrated the heavy metals, harvest, and extract the metals from the biomass.

The limitation of phytoremediation depends on the ability of specific plants to grow in specific contaminated areas. The plant species employed may not be an invasive species. For example, the use of kudzu in the American South which took over the landscape. Plants can only remove toxins as deep as their roots, so the technique might not solve groundwater contamination.

Organic Pesticides

Herbicides:

In recent years, several organic herbicides are for sale. They are all contact herbicides and have no systemic effect. Take care when spraying because they will also burn your crops. They are based on:

20% acetic acid

5% citric acid

55% d-limonene

50% clove oil

45% clove oil + 45% cinnamon oil and

50% lemongrass oil.

Eugenol

2-Phenethyl Propionate

Sodium Lauryl Sulfate

Ammonium Nonanoate

Pelargonic Acid + Fatty Acids

These organic products may be effective in controlling weeds, but have limitations. These organic herbicides can kill weeds that have emerged from the soil. They have no residual activity on weeds emerging afterwards. These herbicides can burn back the tops of perennial weeds, perennial weeds recover quickly.

These organic products are effective in controlling weeds when the weeds are small but are less effective on older plants. In a recent study (Lanini) found that weeds in the cotyledon or first true leaf stage were more susceptible to organic control than older weeds. These organic herbicides work much better when the temperature is above 24°C. Improve the effectiveness of organic herbicides, by thoroughly spraying to a point where the herbicide is running off plant leaf surface.

A classic organic herbicide is made in the following way. Table salt 1 cup, vinegar 5% two cups and four liters of water. If a higher percent of vinegar is available, it will kill the weeds faster.

Organic Fungicides

Baking Soda: 4 teaspoons of Baking Soda, 1 teaspoon of mild liquid soap added to four liters of water.

Copper solutions

Bordeaux Mix: Use latex gloves, goggles, and a dust mask

The homemade recipe for Bordeaux mix is 10-10-100 copper sulfate: dry hydrated lime: water. First prepare your stock solutions.

Step 1. 450 gm lime into 1 gallon of water and let it stand for two hours.

Step 2. Mix1 pound copper in 1 gallon of water. After mixing place in a sealed glass vessel.

Step 3. Fill a large bucket with 2 gallons of water. Add 1 quart of the copper solution. Mix the copper slowly into the water. Then, while stirring add one quart of your lime stock solution. The mixture is now ready to use.

They use various copper compounds as organic fungicides. See uses below: (Table 1).

Table 1.

Metallic copper

Active Ingredient equivalent REI^ PHI*

24% copper oxychloride +

21% copper hydroxide 28% 48 hr 0 days

98% basic copper sulfate 53% 24 hr 0 days

58% copper salts of fatty

and rosin acids 5.14% 12 hr 0 days

77% copper hydroxide 50% 24 hr 0 days

19.8% copper sulfate

Pentahydrate 5% 48 hr 0 days

10% copper octanoate 1.8% 4 hr 0 days

84% cuprous hydroxide 50% 24 hr 0 days

^Restricted Entry Interval

*Pre-Harvest Interval days before the crop eaten

Bordeaux Mix is effective against:

Fire Blight

Potato Blight

Black Spot[1]

Peach Leaf Curl

Downy Mildew

Powdery Mildew

---

1. http://www.bigblogofgardening.com/organic-garden-photos/summer-vegetable-and-flower-garden-images-2010/black-spot-infection-in-pear-tree/

Anthracnose

Late Blight

Rust

Scatter elemental Sulfur powder underneath the plants and on lower leaves. The sulfur fumes rise, killing fungi on contact. To disperse elemental sulfur safely, one must use gloves, face mask and goggles.

Dissolved sulfur (0.4%) as a foliar spray is good against fungal diseases.

Silicon: Multiple Uses

Laing et al. (2006) wrote in his review, "Silicon is a functional plant nutrient. In particular, silicon application can significantly enhance insect pest and disease resistance in plants, with consequent yield increases."

Silicon is abundant and comprises 28% of the earth's crust. Silicon has a catalytic role in the expression of physiological resistance. This is because of its enhancement of the production of tannic and phenolic compounds. Silicon is easy to integrate into management of insect pests and diseases. The chemical leaves no pesticide residues in food and is safe to the environment. Silicon reduces insect and mite populations, but doesn't wipe them out. Employ the silicon with other insecticides to eradicate pest.

Suppliers recommend applying potassium silicate 0.5 to 1% solution (1 liters/ 100 liters of water).

Apply up to the day of harvest (0 day PHI).

Do not apply over 2.5 liters/1000 m^2 per application.

Do not apply over 20 liters/season/

1000m^2.

Not to be used post-harvest.

Laing et al. (2006) found treating vegetables 80mg/l potassium silicate gave excellent results controlling red spider mite. Doubling the amount only gave a slightly better result.

Silicon as a microelement is more important than most people believe. It acts as a catalyst for the uptake of other essential elements, such as calcium, chlorine, fluorine, sodium, sulfur, zinc, aluminum, cobalt, manganese, and others. Plants absorb silicon as silicic acid, H_4SiO_4. Roots take up the silicic acid and transported it through the xylem to stems and leaves. Silicon plays an important role during abiotic and biotic stress of plants (Deshmuhk, et al. 2017).

Plants convert Silicon monomers $(Si(OH_3)O$ into silicate polymers. One finds silicified (accumulated silicon) cells in various stem cells and increase the cells' physical strength (Currie & Perry 2017).

Principal functions of silicon in plants:

A natural defense system in a plant from physiological stress;

Promotes uptake of macro-and microelement important in plant growth and acceleration of metabolic processes;

Ensuring healthy development

Maintains the plant's immune system.

Treat seeds before planting at a rate of 0.5-1.0 liter for ten liters of water to treat one ton of seed.

Silicon treatment during the vegetation period via spraying or irrigation at a recommended quantity of 2-4 treatments during the plant's life cycle. Apply the first spraying during early vegetative phase and then again before flowering. There are those who disagree with its use during flowering. The rate of application is the same throughout the plant's life cycle: 0.25-0.4 l for 1 hectare.

Diseases and Insect Pests

Principles of Plant Protection

Any discussion on plant protection starts with the crop protection triangle.

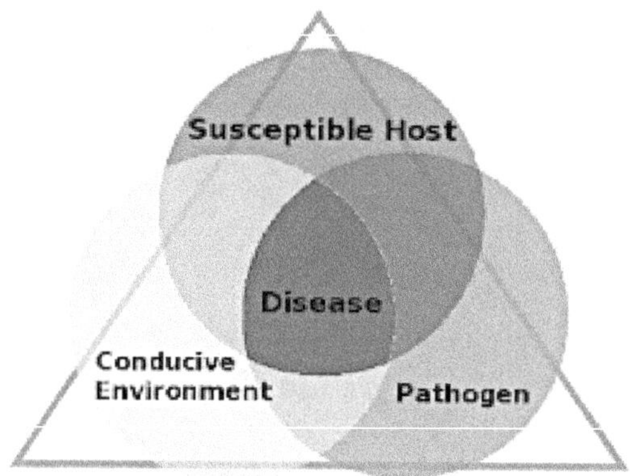

Figure 7. Factors that cause Plant Disease.

To achieve the state of a diseased crop, you need three factors:

A susceptible Host plants

A pathogen

An environment conducive to

Disease development.

Protecting crops fall into two groups-preventive and therapeutic. Most methods are preventive. These include employing resistant varieties, treating plants with a protective chemical, following certain cultural practices, using biological control, and eliminating centers and vectors of infection. The therapeutic method applies toxic substances to the plant to destroy an already established parasite.

Plant pests often cause farmers with serious economic losses. The farmer needs a fast response to his problem. This is where many farmers make their mistakes. Plant protection starts from preparing your fields or greenhouses. Make sure there is no residue from previous crops. Keep the growing area free of weeds.

Some plants like nightshade have infected seed. Several viruses infect Nightshade. Insects feeding on nightshade will pass the viruses to your crop. Cleanliness is the first step in crop protection. Keep the inside and outside of the greenhouse free of weeds.

To catch infestations early is crucial to plant protection. Inspect your crop at least twice a week for pests. Check the underside of the leaves for signs of disease or deleterious insects. If you are planning to use predatory insects as control, don't wait for an infestation. Release the predatory insects into the greenhouse at the start of growth cycle.

To diagnose cannabis diseases can be problematic. Ill-informed growers often misdiagnose. Example: Symptoms- like yellow or wilting leaves[1].

Several reasons could be the cause for plants' bad physiological state. Under-watering or over-watering can cause these symptoms. Yellow and wilted leaves can result from unbalanced pH[2], over fertilization, excessive nutrient burn[3], improper light, or extreme weather.

The only tool you need for identifying pests and diseases is a magnifying glass.

---

1. https://www.royalqueenseeds.com/blog-yellow-cannabis-leaves-n523

2. https://blueskyorganics.com/growing-guides/understanding-soil-ph-a-beginners-guide/

3. https://blueskyorganics.com/growing-guides/growing-cannabis-nutrition-for-beginners/

Fungal Diseases

Gray Mold (Botrytis)

Cannabis is one of the hundreds of plants attacked by Botrytis. Botrytis can attack every part of the cannabis plant. This fungus is most severe during the late stage of flowering on the buds. Botrytis needs high humidity (above 80% RH) to develop.

One can easily detect Botrytis with the naked eye. Prophylactic sprays are the best way to control the disease. If you have an infestation, cut out the damaged parts of the plant and another 15% around the damaged area. Symptoms aren't yet visible in the surrounding tissue. Burn the infected plant material to remove it as a source of continued infestation. Spray with an organic fungicide. It requires prompt action to prevent the entire crop from being destroyed in just a few days. Grey mold is the biggest threat to growing Cannabis.

Early detection of Grey mold is possible before the signs of the characteristic cottony-gray buds. The first signs of a Botrytis are the change in color and texture of the plant. Leaves become dry and stems turn soft and brown.

Other early symptoms of early gray mold are a powdery white substance. This will darken over time to a gray fuzz and eventually turn into a gray-brown slime.

Once the disease is visible to the naked eye, the internal damage to the plant is too far gone for treatment. Remove the infected plants or tissues, to prevent contamination to nearby plants.

Powdery Mildew *Golovinomyces*[1]

Powdery mildew (PM)[2] is a serious cannabis pathogen. PM is easy to identify. The disease appears as a white-gray powdery fungus on the plant surface. Powdery mildew spreads easily from the leaves and plant base, to the bud and flowers. Once infected, it ruins the buds.

The most destructive fungal pathogen in Cannabis is Powdery Mildew. Powdery mildew is an obligate biotroph which invades the vascular cells of the

---

1. *https://apsjournals.apsnet.org/doi/full/10.1094/PDIS-04-18-0586-PDN*

2. https://www.medicinalgenomics.com/powdery-mildew/

plant and can remain invisible. Under ideal conditions, powdery mildew has a 4–7-day invisible inoculation window while it builds an internal network.

The powdery mildew vascularized network in cannabis can be detected by expensive PCR DNA based tests, not an expense worthwhile for a small greenhouse. Later stage powdery mildew infection and conidiospore generation spread rapidly to other plants. The disease emerges and sporulates 2 weeks into flowering thus destroying a mature crop.

Powdery mildew hinders the plant's ability to absorb essential nutrients. This weakens the plant and makes it more susceptible to the disease.

Prevention[3] is the best method to control PM, which thrives in cool, humid environments. Avoid overcrowding and excess irrigation. One must maintain a sanitary growth space with good airflow. Clean equipment between crops and if used in the same field. Infection is sometimes inevitable. Monitor young plants and leaves for blistering and strange odors. These are the signs precede the white powder. If prevention fails, several organic treatments for powdery mildew are available[4].

---

3. http://www.questclimate.com/powdery-mildew/

4. https://moldresistantstrains.com/6-ways-cure-powdery-mildew-cannabis-organically/

Fusarium

The soil-dwelling fungus, Fusarium, which causes either Fusarium root rot, Fusarium wilt or both. Fusarium blocks the uptake of nutrients to the plant, causing systematic death. The disease causes wilt and dark spots appear on lower leaves. These spots become yellow to brown. Afterwards, the leaves droop, but don't fall off. If untreated, this pattern will repeat itself up the plant.

When Fusarium causes root rot, its symptoms are unseen until its damage is visible. The roots of the plant turn red. This coloration moves up the stem. The stem will burst open in one or more places. This allows secondary infection by insects and other diseases. This finishes with the death of the plant.

Verticilium

Verticilium wilt symptoms are similar to those of Fusarium. Verticilium wilt causes yellowing of leaves at the bottom of the plant with yellowing leaves. The yellowing begins in the veins and leaf margins.

Affected leaves darken in appearance and wilt. The adjacent stem will also darken and weaken at the base. Verticilium Wilt happen in larger sections at once with Verticilium as compared to branch by branch with Fusarium.

Bacterial Diseases

Bacteria blight: *Pseudomonas syringae pv. cannabina* and *Striatura ulcerosa*

Bacterial blight is the most common bacterial disease in Cannabis. Its symptoms are like the fungal disease, brown leaf spot.

The disease develops best in wet, cool conditions—optimum temperatures for disease are between 12 to 25°C. The bacteria spread via the seeds and dispersed between plants by rain.

Recommendations: Fixed copper compounds (such as Bordeaux and copper hydroxide), streptomycin (an antibiotic), and coordination productions (such as Bravo CM) registered and employed against *Pseudomonas syringae* with various degrees of success.

Uncommon bacterial diseases

There are three uncommon bacterial diseases in Cannabis. Crown gall by *Agrobacterium tumefaciens*, bacterial wilt by *Erwinia tracheiphila*, xanthomonas leaf spot by *Xanthomonas campestris pv. Cannabis*. Crown gall is world famous because researchers used its bacteriophage for genetic engineering.

Agrobacterium tumefaciens causes tumors on various plant parts. Crown gall begins initially as small swellings on the root or stem near the soil line. It can also start on the upper stems. Other symptoms are stunting and chlorotic leaves.

Erwinia tracheiphila–Bacterial wilt first appears as a drooping or wilting of one or more leaves on the plant. Afterwards, the entire plant wilts. Rapid plant death follows. Sometimes the disease causes excessive stunting of the plant. This causes excessive blooming and branching.

Xanthomonas campestris prefers temperature at 25-30 C, but is inactive at temperatures below 10 C. *Xanthomonas* can live in a soil for over a year and spread by water movement. This includes rain, irrigation and surface water. It also causes black rot, which is black lesions on the plant surface.

Viruses

Researchers have studied a limited number of viruses in cannabis. The two cannabis-specific viruses are: the hemp streak virus (HSV) and the hemp mosaic virus (HMV). The virus is spread by viral vectors including aphids and whiteflies.

While it's primarily target is tobacco, evidence exists that tobacco mosaic virus (TMV) infects Cannabis. The hemp mosaic virus HMV is in reality the cowpea strain of TMV.

The tobacco mosaic virus is a common plant virus effecting numerous plants species. It is a thermostable virus. TMV can withstand temperatures to 4 kc. Ideal climatic conditions[1] for the dispersal of the disease is low humidity and high temperatures.

TMV symptoms include interveinal chlorosis on young growth. Don't confuse this with a nutrient deficiency. Leaves have contrasting dark and light spots and wrinkling, slightly lumpy leaves which gets worse as the disease progresses.

Necrotic spots appear, growth becoming stunted develop, and the base of the plant weakens quickly in hot dry climates.

Other viruses that affect cannabis plants to a lesser degree are the tobacco streak virus (TSV), the tobacco ringspot virus (TRSV), the alfalfa mosaic virus (AMV) and the cucumber mosaic virus (CMV), which spread aided by viral vectors[2] like seeds and aphids. Arabis mosaic virus (ArMV) spreads through seeds and nematodes. It can cause asymptomatic infections with no visible signs on the plant.

---

1. https://www.dinafem.org/en/blog/air-circulation-for-cannabis-growing/

2. https://www.dinafem.org/en/blog/common-pest-cannabis-plants/

Insect Pests

Aphids and Ants

There 4,400 species of aphids in the family Aphididae. Two hundred and fifty aphid species are serious pests for agriculture[1] and forestry[2]. Aphids vary in length from 1 to 10 millimeters.

There are various kinds of Aphids. Aphids are sucking insects. They suck the sap of plants and secrete a substance called honeydew. This sticky resin is high in sugars and a favorite food of ants and fungi. Often one finds the leaves of the vegetables cover with black mildew where aphids feed. Ants "milk" the aphids by stroking their abdomen. The relationship between aphids and ants is symbiotic. The ants protect the aphids and the aphids provide food for the ants.

Recent scientific studies have found that aphids protect ants from predators, such as lacewings and ladybugs. Ants also protect the aphids from a fungal infection that are lethal, by removing the bodies of the infected aphids.

If you see numerous ants on a tree or plant, there is a high probably of a large infestation of aphids. Many ant species farm ants.

Aphid's honeydew (a sweet excretion as a result of sucking the sap of the plant) provides food for ants. The aphids allow ants to relocate them.

The control of ants is one way of regulating the aphid population. Ant bait traps are an effective means of control, since ants take the bait back to the colony. The bait kills more ants in the colony. A smaller ant population opens the aphids to predators.

Wrap Sticky tape around trees to catch the ants. Wash aphids off the leaves with organic soapy water sprays or neem oil.

---

1. https://en.wikipedia.org/wiki/Agriculture

2. https://en.wikipedia.org/wiki/Forestry

Red Spider Mites

Spider mites attack and feast on hundreds of different plants. They begin their infestation on the undersides of plant leaves. They spin silk webs to protect themselves against the elements and predators.

Red Spider mites are less than 1 millimeter (0.04 inches) in size and are red or black. They prefer hot, dry conditions. Red Spider mites lay transparent eggs that hatch in as little as three days.

Red Spider mites mature sexually within five days, and female mites can live for up to two to four weeks. The female can lay, twenty eggs per day.

Spider mites cause damage by puncturing plant cells to feed. Spider mites attack both indoor and outdoor plants. Their colonies grow rapidly and if uncontrolled wreak havoc on the growth of the plant in the vegetative state and destroy buds during bloom.

Initial symptoms of spider mite infection are:

Tiny spots or stippling on leaves (caused by feeding)

Thin, silky webs surrounding the underside of plant leaves and branches.

Larger infestations cause leaves to turn yellow, become limp and eventually, die. Uncontrolled colonies will kill your plants and or lower your yields and quality of the buds.

Fungus Gnats

The adult flying fungus gnats are easy to observe. The adults don't cause damage. Their larvae have a separate name: root maggots. They live in the soil and feed on the roots. The flying adult gnats spread the infestation quickly.

Root maggots feed on the roots. Evidence of their presence comes after they have done damage. They weaken the plant by reducing the root mass. The plant manifests this as deficiencies in nutrients and water.

If you dig at the base of your plants, you can expose the presence of the root maggots.

Whiteflies

Whiteflies[1] are one of the major scourges of agriculture. Unlike most insects that carry one or two viruses, Whiteflies can carry numerous viruses and often over one at a time. It is the vector for hemp mosaic virus (HMV). They are a major pest in Cucurbits and Solanaceae. If the whitefly is present, shaking a Cannabis plant will make a cloud of them to rise off the plant. Whitefly suck nutrients of the leaf and leave mottled spots much like the mite damage. They are easy to identify.

Light attracts whitefly. Many commercial vegetable growers spray at night with flood lamps which draws the whitefly from the plant canopy.

---

1. https://www.maximumyield.com/the-war-on-whiteflies/2/1368

Thrips

Thrips are tiny (0.8mm) flying insect. They suck leaves, leaving silvery marks on the leaves, sometimes with "dots". Damaged Leaves often become brittle. To identify thrips before damage becomes evident, one needs to use monitoring traps and inspect them regularly.

Caterpillars

Caterpillars are the larval stage of Lepidoptera (butterflies and moths). They are ravenous and chew on leaves and stems. Large infestations can strip the leaves off a plant in a short time. Their sizes range from less than a centimeter to five to eight centimeters. They color vary, but most take on a green color from the large amounts of chlorophyll they consume. In several countries in the Far East, they eat the larger caterpillars.

It is easy to identify their damage from the chew on leaf margins or holes in the leaves.

Snails and slugs

Snail and slugs are rarely a problem in well-sealed greenhouses. They eat the leaves of cannabis and leave a slimy, silvery, mucus- trail, making their identification easy.

Leaf miners

Leaf miners are very tiny worms rarely seen on marijuana plants until the damage is visible. They feed on cannabis inner leaf tissue. They mine tunnels in the leaf. The leaf will appear with squiggly white or silvery lines across the center of the leaves.

Borers

Borers are probably the worst pests in hemp fields. Two worse borers are the European corn borer (*Ostrinia nubilalis*), and the hemp borer (*Grapholita delineana*). European corn borers (ECBs). ECBs are native to Eastern Europe. *Cannabis sativa* and *Humulus lupulus* (hops) were their original host plants. ECBs switched to maize after Zea mays cultivation began two hundred thirty years in Europe (Nagy 1976, 1986). ECB feeding Stem cankers result from ECB feeding. They reduce the structural integrity of the stems. Stems with weighty flowering tops break at cankers. Large boring worms into the secondary stems causes wilting of distal plant parts. Heavy infestations collapse entire plants.

ECB entry holes in stems are open wounds, providing access for other insects or fungi. ECBs hatching late in the season may infest flowering tops instead of stems, where they spin webs and scatter feces.

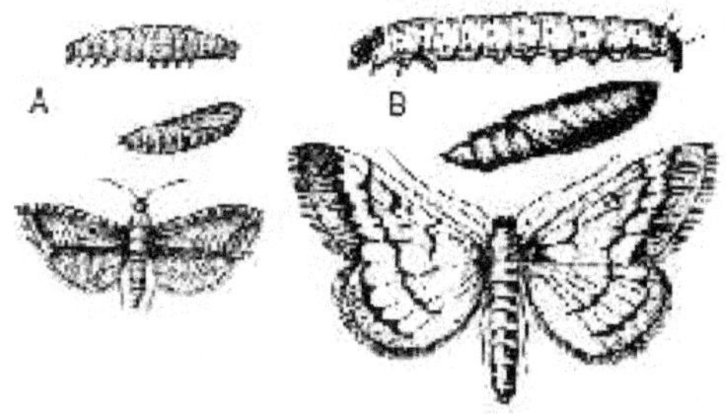

Figure 8. Larva, pupa and female moth of *Grapholita delineana* (A) compared to larger *Ostrinia nubilalis* (B). Both 1.5 times actual size.

European Corn Borers are larger than the hemp borers (HBs) (Figure 1). HBs induce comparable stem damage. They are much more destructive in flowering tops. HBs are also known as hemp leaf rollers and hemp seed eaters. HBs have destroyed 80% of a crop's flowering tops and eaten significant amounts of seed crops. HBs appear host-specific on Cannabis (Mushtaque et al. 1973),

Other Cannabis caterpillars cause damage like stem borers (e.g., *Cossus cossus, Zeuzera multistrigata, Papaipema nebris, P. cataphracta,* and *Endocylyta excrescens*). Some caterpillars damage leaves, seeds, and flowering tops (e.g., *Mamestra brassicae, Autographa gamma, Melanchra persicariae, Spilosoma obliqua, Arctia caja,* and *Loxostege sticticalis*). Few caterpillars induce damage like ECBs and HBs. The budworm (e.g., *Heliothis armigera* and *Heliothis viriplaca*) wreak havoc on flowering buds, but leave stems alone.

Other stem boring insects include the grubs of flea beetles (*Phyllotreta nemorum*), tumbling flower beetles (Mordellistena *micans* and *M. parvula*), longhorn beetles (*Thyestes gebleri*), weevils (*Ceutorhynchus rapae* and *Rhinocus pericarpius*), and the maggots of gall midges (*Melanogromyza urticivora*).

Nematodes

Nematodes are microscopic in unsegmented worms, of the Phylum *Nematoda*. Plant-parasitic nematodes attack many crops and plants in your garden. Nematodes feed mainly on the roots of plants.

Damage shows up as stunted and nodulated roots. This stunts plant growth and if infestation is high can kill the plant.

Nematodes only move short distances under their own power. Nematodes spread through poor sanitation and movement of infected soil and planting material. Place all infected plants in cardboard boxes to dry out and then burn them. Clean tools with soap and water outside of the greenhouse. Clean your shoes of any soil before entering or leaving the greenhouse.

Nutrients: Deficiencies and Excesses

The two figures below are a guide for growers to determine the level their

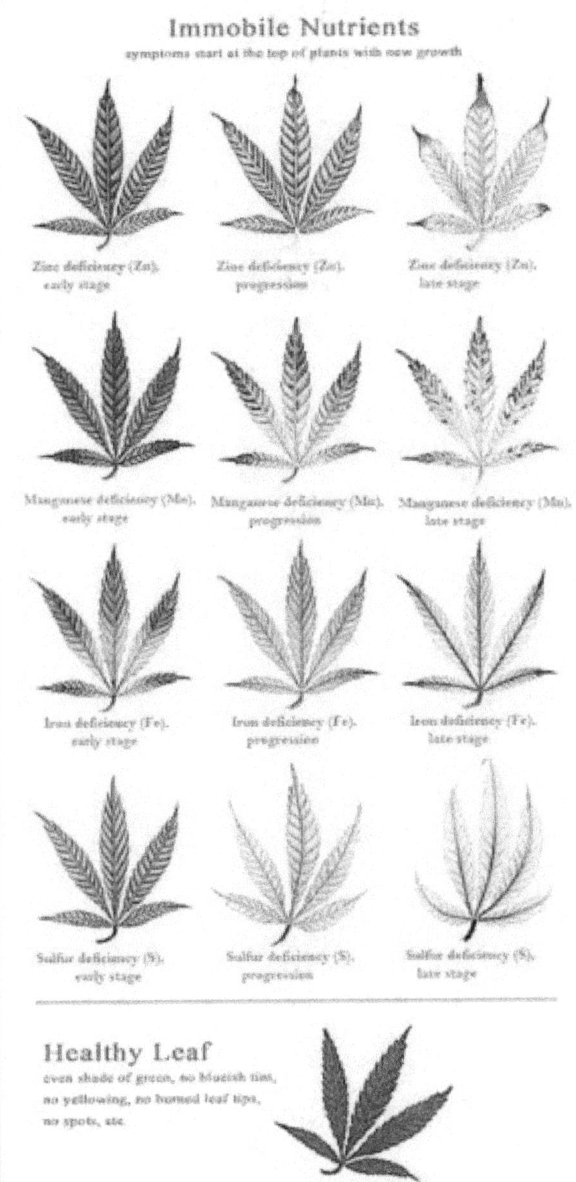

plant's health.

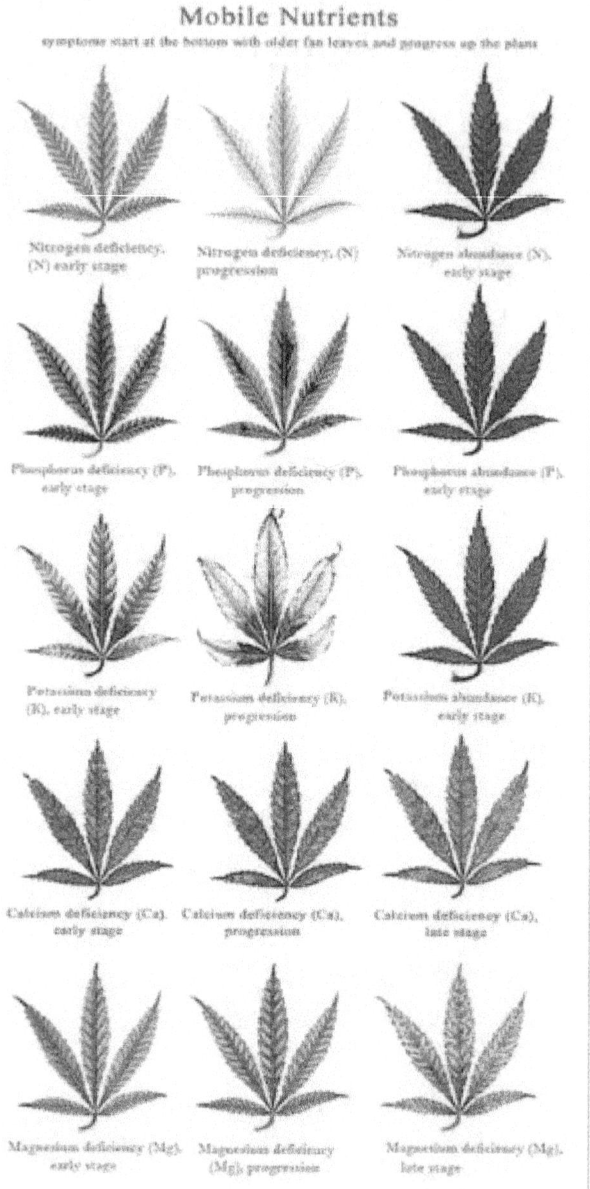

It is important to keep these charts with you when you examine your plants daily.

Organic Insecticides

Equipment needed for Plant Protection.

1. 10-20 liter back sprayer.

2. Goggles

3. Latex Gloves

4. Plastic Spraying Pants and Jacket

5. Spraying mask

6. Plastic Graduated Cylinder 250 ml

7. Plastic Graduated Measuring Cup 500-1000 ml.

8. Simple Kitchen Scale up to 2kg

9. Liter Bucket

10. Tablespoon

As you will learn below, not all organic pesticides are safe to humans. Please use the safety equipment.

Bordeaux Mix,

Copper sulfate and lime mixed in water is good against snails and slugs.

Neem

In India, they have used natural plant extract from ancient times. Neem oil is a powerful, all-natural plant extract for warding off pests. In fact, neem juice is the most powerful natural pesticide on the planet, holding over 50 natural insecticides. You can use this extremely bitter tree leaf to make a natural pesticide spray.

Make neem oil spray by adding 1/2 an ounce of high-quality organic neem oil and ½ teaspoon of a mild organic liquid soap to two quarts of warm water. Stir slowly. It should be use immediately.

Salt Spray

For treating plants infested with spider mites, mix two tablespoons of Himalayan Crystal Salt[1] into one gallon of warm water and spray on infected areas.

Mineral Oil

Mix 10-30 ml of high-grade oil with one liter of water. Mix thoroughly Stir and add to a spray bottle. This organic pesticide works well for dehydrating insects and their eggs.

Citrus Oil and Cayenne Pepper

This mixture works well on ants. Mix 10 drops of citrus essential oil with one teaspoon cayenne pepper and 1 cup of warm water. Mix well and spray the affected areas.

Soap, Orange Citrus Oil, and Water

To make this natural pesticide mix three tablespoons of liquid Organic Castile soap with 1 ounce of Orange oil to one gallon of water. Shake well. This is an especially effective treatment against slugs. You can spray it directly on ants and roaches.

Eucalyptus Oil

A great natural pesticide for flies, bees, and wasps. Sprinkle a few drops of eucalyptus oil on locations with insects. The smell will drive them away.

Onion and Garlic Spray

Mince one clove of garlic and one medium-sized onion. Add to a quart of water. Wait one hour and then add one teaspoon of cayenne pepper and one

---

1. http://www.globalhealingcenter.com/natural-health/himalayan-crystal-salt-benefits/

tablespoon of liquid soap to the mix. This organic spray will hold its potency for one week if stored in the refrigerator.

Chrysanthemum Flower Tea

These flowers hold a powerful plant chemical component called pyrethrum. This substance invades the nervous system of insects, rendering them immobile. You can make your own spray by boiling 100 grams of dried flowers into 1 liter of water. Make this extract in a well-aerated place, use latex gloves, and a mask. Even though organic, pyrethrum is poisonous to humans.

Boil dried flowers in water for twenty minutes. Strain, cool, and pour into a spray bottle. You can store the mixture for up to two months. You can also add some organic neem oil to enhance the effectiveness.

Tobacco Spray

Just as tobacco is hazardous to humans, tobacco spray was once a commonly used pesticide for killing pests, caterpillars, and aphids. Mix one cup of organic tobacco (select a brand that is organic and all-natural) into 4 liters of water. Allow the mixture to set overnight. After 24-hours, the mix should have a light brown color. If very dark, add more water. You can use this mixture on most plants, except those in the solanaceous family (tomatoes, peppers, eggplants, etc.)

Chile Pepper / Diatomaceous Earth

Grind two handfuls of dry chilies into a fine powder and mix with 1 cup of Diatomaceous earth. Add to 2 liters of water and let set overnight. Shake well before applying.

Bacillus Thuringiensis is a bacterium referred to as Bt. These bacteria are a biological pesticide which can kill a large variety of worms, moths and beetles.

Beauveria Bassiana is a fungus that infects aphids, caterpillars, grasshoppers, ants and other insects. It replicates until it kills its host. Therefore, concentration is important. *Beauveria* can't provide an immediate answer to insect infestations. When insects come into contact with *Beaurveria* its spores stick to the insect and germinate. The germinating spores produce enzymes that dissolve the insect cuticle, allowing the fungus to penetrate and grow within the insect's body, killing it. It should be used prophylactically for best results.

Kaolin Clay is a clay. Spray it as a suspension in water on annual plants. It protects against mites, insects, fungi, and harmful bacteria. Use Kaolin Clay as a powder on trees and bushes. It forms a protective layer between the plants and the pests.

Neem Oil is a brown oil with an unpleasant taste and smell. It acts as a repellent for insects and is non-toxic to humans or honey bees.

Plant Oils from citrus, canola, mustard, castor and soybean can kill or repel insects.

Treatment for Nematodes

Select varieties that have nematode resistance. This means that the nematodes will not attack your plants. Tolerant varieties mean the nematodes attack the plant roots, but with limited damage.

As mentioned above clean your shoes on entering and leaving the greenhouse.

Use crop rotation of species resistant to nematodes.

Solarization. Various forms of heat decrease nematode populations, other harmful organisms and weed seeds. Apply heat as pasteurization, steaming, or solarization of the soil before planting. Solarization is the most practical of the three.

Place your drip irrigation lines as if you growing a crop.

Wet the soil.

Cover the soil with clear plastic. The trapped light heats the soil to temperatures damaging to most living organisms. Black, opaque, or translucent plastics are not suitable for solarization. Thin, transparent plastic sheets achieve the best results. Katan (1981) recommended plastic between 25 to 30 μm thick. If the weather is hot, temperatures can rise to between 35°C and 60°C.

(Katan 1981). Soil temperatures rise to effective levels in the first 10 to 30 cm of soil (Katan 1987), and even in this range temperatures drop off as depth increases.

Place dirt around the edges of the plastic sheet to seal the area.

Water the soil every four to five days. The heat under the plastic converts the water to steam.

Keep the soil cover for at least four weeks.

Biological Control.

Biological control is the management of plant-pests by living organisms. Bacteria, fungi, predatory nematodes, and other invertebrates have been employed for control of nematodes. You can build up biological control by supporting the growth of beneficial organisms via various soil amendments. Control by beneficial soil organisms is limited. *Pasteuria* species, which are bacterial parasites of various plant-parasitic nematodes occurring naturally in Florida soils. Weibelzahl-Fulton et al. (1996) showed in a seven-year experiment with tobacco that nematode species *Meloidgyne incognita* and *M. javanica Pasteuria penetrans* (a group of bacteria) suppressed exclusively these two species of nematodes. Tobacco plants treated with *P. penetrans* had fewer galls, egg masses, and eggs than plants that lacked the biological control agent. Nematode-trapping fungi have been studied as potential candidates for biological control (Wang and McSorley 2003). Their adhesive knobs, rings, or net structures trap nematodes and kill them. Other types of fungi may parasitize nematode eggs. Neither fungi nor *Pasteuria* spp. are available for widespread commercial use at this moment. But they can be found in a healthy soil environment, as can predators such as mites and predatory nematodes. Recent research has shown that a wide range of nematode natural enemies occur in Florida soils Most biological predators are generalists. This meaning they feed on various species during their lifetime. Generalist predators are a disadvantage for biological control. They will not only feed on the targeted pest, but on other suitable prey for them, which may include beneficial organisms. When there is insufficient food available, they disperse, allowing the pest to recover.

On the positive side, generalist predators can lower the populations of several pests at one time. No predators are commercially available for nematodes (Krueger & McSorley, 2018).

Indicator Plants

Indicator plants are plants that help the farmer determine insect or viral infestation before it becomes an economic disaster.

Thrips carry TSWV (Tomato Wilt Spot Virus) and INSV (Impatiens Necrotic Spot Virus). Thrips prefer Petunias and fava bean to other plants if available. Therefore, farmers plant throughout their greenhouse 5-10 plants of Petunias and fava beans. Since the thrips feed on the petunias and fava beans first, then regular inspection of these plants will allow the farmer to catch the infestation before it damages to his crop.

Tagetes (marigold) is another such plant. While it can control root-knot nematodes red spider mite prefer Tagetes over all other plants. You will see the webs of the red spider mite on the Tagetes several days before it attacks your crop. They report Rosemary oil to be an alternative spray to kill red spider mites.

Dangerous pesticides approved by Organic Growers Associations.

Because something is organic, doesn't mean it is safe to humans. You need to wash organic fruits and vegetables the same as conventionally grown. LD50 means the dose that will kill 50% of the test organisms. The lower the LD50 the more dangerous the compound is to living organisms. The figure is milligrams of compound to kilograms of body weight. Below is a partial list of dangerous chemicals approved by US organic grower association.

Pyrethrum (LD50 of 200 mg/kg) is a natural botanical pesticide. They make it from the dried flowers, *Chrysanthemum cinerariifolium* and *Chrysanthemum coccineum*. Exposure to low doses may lead to injuriousness results in cats. Humans exposed to high levels of pyrethrum may cause symptoms such as asthmatic breathing, sneezing, nasal stuffiness, headache, nausea, loss of coordination, tremors, convulsions, facial flushing, and swelling.

Organic farmers use Boron (LD50 of 560 mg/kg) as a fertilizer. Protracted exposure or ingestion of boron residues have a negative effect on the brain, liver and heart. The long-term effects of boron (via ingestion, skin absorption, or absorption from body cavities or mucous membranes) induces anorexia, weight loss, vomiting, mild diarrhea, skin rash, alopecia, convulsions, and anemia.

Acetic Acid (LD50 3310 mg/kg). Organic farmers use acetic acid at high concentrations (90% and above). It is mixed with soap and Epsom salts to create an herbicide. At this concentration they classify it as corrosive to the skin. If used without proper safety equipment, it will cause skin burns and damage to your eyes.

Copper sulfate (LD50: 300 mg/kg) is a well-known fungicide and insecticide. Its synthetic equivalent has an LD50 of 4500mg/kg (Mancozeb).

Rotenone (LD50: 132 mg/kg) struck from the list of approved organic pesticides it has been reinstated. www. thefarmersdaughterusa.

com/2013/06/organic-pesticides.html.

Nicotine sulfate (LD50: 50-60 mg/kg) controls aphids, thrips, mites and other insects. It is an organic neurotoxin that interferes with the transmitter substance between nerves and muscles.

Mycorrhiza

Mycorrhiza are fungi that grow with plant roots in a symbiotic relationship.

Mycorrhizae form a network of filaments in the soil and around plant roots. They draw nutrients from the soil that the root system can't access. This fungus-plant symbiosis stimulates plant growth and increases root growth.

There are two types of mycorrhiza fungi: ectomycorrhizal and endomycorrhizal fungi.

Ectomycrrhiza develop only on the exterior of root cells. *Endomycorrhiza* penetrate the plant cells and there are direct metabolic exchanges. We find mostly Ectomycorrhizae on trees. They form visible structures along the roots. Endomycorrhizal fungi colonize the roots of trees, shrubs and most herbaceous plants and don't form visible structures.

Mycorrhizal fungi increase plant tolerance to various environmental stresses. These fungi are essential in soil aggregation process and stimulate microbial activity. Mycorrhizae provide the following benefits to the plants and the environment:

Produce more vigorous plants

Increase plant establishment and survival at seeding or transplanting

Increase yields and crop quality

Improve drought tolerance, allowing watering reduction

Enhance flowering and fruiting

Optimize fertilizers use, especially phosphorus

Increase tolerance to soil salinity

Reduce disease occurrence

Contribute to maintain soil quality and nutrient cycling

Contribute to control soil erosion

Trichoderma species.

Two of the methods in which *Trichoderma* protect plants from pathogenic fungi are hyperparasitism and antibiosis. Hyperparasitism occurs when *Trichoderma* comes into contact with other fungi. It penetrates the fungi and ultimately destroys them.

Trichoderma has developed mechanisms that allow it to identify other pathogenic fungi. The *Trichoderma* then attacks and destroys the other fungi. After penetration into pathogenic fungi, *Trichoderma* release lytic enzymes that degrade the cell structures of the pathogen.

Antibiosis is the release of secondary metabolites that inhibit other parasitic fungi. This prevents them from becoming active parasites and sometimes even kills them.

In addition, these metabolites are also active against various bacteria and virus that may pose a threat to the fungi.

Arbuscular mycorrhizas (AM = fungus plus root) aid plants in phosphorus acquisition from the soil. AM fungi are obligate symbionts, belonging to the phylum *Glomeromycota*. An example being *Glomus macrocarpum*. They form a mutual symbiosis with 80% of land plant species, including several agricultural crops. They provide the host plant with mineral nutrients and water, in exchange for photosynthetic products (Smith and Read, 2008[1]).

Companies sell mycorrhiza.

Follow the instructions of how to prepare the solution in a ten-liter bucket.

Let the solution stand for 15-20 minutes before using it.

Remove rooted cutting from their seedling trays and place into the 10 L bucket for 20-40 seconds to allow mycorrhiza to coat the roots.

Remove the treated rooted cuttings and place in a clean dry 10 L bucket.

1. https://www.frontiersin.org/articles/10.3389/fmicb.2015.01559/full#B110

Plant immediately into your growing system.

Irrigation Needs

There have not been sufficient studies conducted on the water usage of Cannabis plants. A rule of thumb is to have available 12 to 16.5 liters/square meter of growing area per day as a peak use rate for the hottest day. For example, a 6-meter x 4-meter net growing area is 24 sq. meters. At peak requirement you need to irrigate at a rate of 288 to 396 liters per day. This corresponds with the evapotranspiration rate for most areas of the country. The following factors can increase or decrease the amount of water needed:

Radiation-high radiation causes an increase in water needs.

Shade- reduces transpiration and reduces water needs.

Air movement- Increases transpiration and increases water needs.

Plant Size- As the plant grows it needs more water.

Leaching- this is adding extra water to wash out excess salts in your growing media.

Type of Irrigation-the efficiency of the irrigation system will alter the amount of water you use.

Water quality-Water with high electric conductivity (EC measures the amount of salts in the water) will require leaching the soil.

If you have a scale there is a simple method to determine water needs. Thoroughly water the plants in the morning and let them drain for at least 30 minutes. Then weigh the pots, come back 24 hours later and weigh the pots again. The decrease in weight is the amount of water the plant has used. Water use will differ from day to day.

Even in artificial media systems, irrigation signifies a large and potentially important loss of nutrients. Irrigation is also a source of environmental pollution. A surplus of 20% to 50% of the plant's water uptake in each irrigation cycle is often recommended. Annual use of irrigation water ranges from 150 to 200 mm (e.g., leafy vegetable) in soil-based greenhouse crops to 1000 to 1500 mm in soilless-grow) For container nursery production, as cited by Fulcher et al., those values could be as high as 2900 mm excess nutrient solution enters the ground water.

Tensiometers

A tensiometer measures soil moisture. The tensiometer measures the tension that plants' roots must apply to remove water from the soil. The tension measured by the tensiometer is a direct measure of the availability of water to a plant. You can employ tensiometers in any irrigated crop either outdoors or under protected culture. They provide data to aid the grower in his irrigation decisions. With crops that have high water requirements or where any wilting will damage yields, tensiometers are an excellent aid to irrigation needs.

Insert the tensiometers into the soil at the midpoint of the main fibrous root system. Their irrigation water will wet the soil and at the bottom of the root zone.

Correct placement is crucial. Placed too deep in a shallow rooted crop and the readings will cause you to irrigate too late, thus causing water stress. Improper placement in a deep-rooted crop, will cause unnecessary irrigation and water logging. To avoid excessive irrigation, place the tensiometer at the bottom of the root zone to check subsoil moisture and drainage.

Relative Humidity

Relative Humidity is the amount of water vapor present in air expressed as a percentage of the amount needed for saturation at the same temperature. Plants absorb carbon dioxide from the atmosphere. They must open their stomata to capture the atmospheric carbon dioxide. At the same time the stomata are open water vapor escapes (evapotranspiration). A water gradient develops, and the plant absorbs water via its roots and translocates it to the leaves. When the plant absorbs water, it absorbs nutrients from the growing media. If the humidity left unbalanced, then:

1. At low humidity, the plant draws water from the soil at a high rate. Under these conditions the plant can't absorb water at a rate equal to loss through the stomatal openings. This results in closure of the stomata. Low humidity reduces CO2 availability, which limits the photosynthetic process. This leads to stress, slow growth and compromised yield. With extreme low humidity, the plant wilts and dies because it cannot offset the water stress imposed by the lack of atmospheric water.

2. High humidity causes a low water gradient between the plant and atmosphere. This reduces nutrient uptake efficiency, which can lead to nutrient deficiencies. Calcium is very susceptible to this phenomenon.

A saturated growing media's pH drops resulting roots unable to absorb nutrients.

Optimal Relative Humidity Rates

Cloning: 70%-75% RH

Vegetation: 65%-70% RH

Flower: 60%-65% RH

Night phase of flower: 55%-60% RH

Additional CO2

CO2

Prior et al. 2011 wrote, "Empirical records provide incontestable evidence for the global rise in carbon dioxide (CO_2) concentration in the earth's atmosphere. Elevated CO_2 levels stimulates plant growth, photosynthesis increases, and economic yield is often enhanced. The application of more CO_2 can increase plant water use efficiency and result in less water use."

Chandra et al. 2011 used two concentrations of elevated CO_2 (545 and 700 μmol mol^{-1}). They found that 545 umol mol^{-1} had no significant positive effect on Cannabis growth. They concluded, "the effects of elevated CO_2 concentrations on *Cannabis sativa* varieties were significant, leading to an increase in net photosynthesis and water use efficiency of this species. However, the magnitude of the increase was 'variety-specific'."

Elevated CO_2 levels allows cannabis to grow at higher temperatures and utilize higher light intensities. Increase light intensity causes increased heat, especially in high-intensity discharge illuminated environments. Both factors alter the photosynthetic system into increased rates, and CO_2 enrichment allows it to run even faster. Pushing CO_2 too hard with light and/or temperature can send your plants into stress.

The current advice is to enhance vegetative growth with CO_2 at a maximum of 800 ppm and bloom with in the 1,200-1,600-ppm range.

Growing Medicinal Cannabis

There are two groups of Cannabis: daylength sensitive and auto-flowering. Daylength sensitive varieties require 18 hours of light for their vegetative stage. The trigger to induce flowering is reducing the daylength to 12 hours. Auto-flowering types came from genes from *Cannabis ruderalis.* These types initiate flowers because of time and not daylength. They are daylength insensitive. Experts recommend a regime of 18 hours for auto-flowering types to make them grow faster. Most auto-flowering varieties will bloom after 2-4 weeks depending on the variety.

Auto-flowering types range from 40 to 70 cm in height grown indoors and can reach 100 cm outdoors. They are small compact plants. Yields can be obtained in as short as 8-9 weeks. Since their entire growth cycle is short, one can grow more cycles/year.

Auto-flowering types being light insensitive don't require an expensive black out system in your greenhouse. They aren't conducive to vegetative propagation as there is no way to extend the vegetative state. This results in a minute amount of cuttings from each mother plant.

Germinating Auto-flowering seeds

Prime your seed before planting them.

Equipment and Supplies

Chlorine (3%)

Glass vessel

Forceps

70% Alcohol

Candle and matches

Seedling tray with peat moss.

Closed rooting box

Dilute the chlorine 3:1

Wash your glass vessel with soap and water, rinse. Then add dilute chlorine to the glass vessel to sterilize it. Leave the chlorine for five minutes and they wash it out thoroughly.

Remove the seed from their packet and place in small mesh bag and tie it closed.

Soak the seeds in the dilute chlorine for ten minutes.

Pour off the Chlorine solution and wash several times. Then leave the seeds under a light amount of running tap water for ten minutes to ensure the chlorine has dissipated.

Leave the seeds in the water for 24 hrs.

Hydrate the peat moss in the seedling tray and allow excess water to drain. Make a small shallow indentation in each individual cell.

Light candle and dip forceps into 70% alcohol and place forceps into the flame to sterilize them.

Use sterilized forceps to pick up a seed and place into a cell of the seedling tray.

Plant seeds only twice their diameter, deep.

Cover the seeds with moist peat moss.

Place seedling tray into rooting box and add a small amount of water to the bottom to maintain the humidity.

Water the tray once a day lightly. Remove excess water.

Once sprouted seeds emerge remove the plastic top of the seedling tray. High humidity at this point is a perfect environment for fungal diseases to develop.

Growing Mother Plants

One problem with using mother plants is somatic mutations. Somatic mutations are "genetic alteration acquired by a somatic cell that passes to the progeny of the mutated cell in the course of cell division. The difference between somatic mutations and germ-line mutations, are germ-line mutations are inherited genetic alterations that occur in the germ cells (i.e., sperm and eggs)."

Ultraviolet radiation, from the sun causes somatic mutations. The longer the exposure the more mutations the plant accumulates. That is why after several generations of using the same mother plants the resulting plants aren't the same as the original cuttings. The rate of somatic mutations from tissue culture-derived plants is slower than propagation material-derived from greenhouse mother plants.

Your mother plants are the genetic source of your production plants. You can purchase clone plants with a particular cannabinoid and terpene profile or you can buy seed. The vast majority of seed available aren't uniform. You will need a minimum of ten seeds. Germinate the seeds and grow up the plants in a vegetative state (18 hours of daylength) for two months. Take ten cuttings and root them from each seedling. Then change the daylength. They will need 12-hour daylength to flower. Once the flowers are ready, stage a large sample of the flowers, dry and cure them, and then send them for analysis. Hopefully, one of the plants from seed will provide you with the chemical profile you are seeking.

One can maintain Mother plants for up to 12 months. The number of clones you need for each season will decide the size pot you want to grow your mother plants in. A good soil mix is 20% volcanic rock, 40% coco peat and 40% peat moss.

Any variation of 20-20-20 (NPK) is good for maintaining mother plants. See below for the amount of nitrogen the plants require. The best way to give fertilizer is in a proportional manner with your water. If you are watering three times a day, give the fertilizer during the first two irrigations and the last only water to wash out any excess salts.

Mother plants must be maintained insect and disease-free Spray prophylactically against Botrytis, red spider mite, and aphids. Insect infestations and diseases can be easily spread via rooted cuttings.

Preparation of Clones

Cannabis cuttings root easily. Depending on the time of year, temperature and humidity the cuttings root from as little as eight to fifteen days.

Equipment list for making clones.

Mother plants

Small pruning shears or a strong scissor.

A watertight vessel 8-10 cm

Water

Cutting board

Alcohol

Cotton wool

Scalpel

Seedling trays with peat moss

Rooting compound

Scissors

Garbage bin

Selecting the correct stems for propagation is crucial to success. Select apical meristems that have stems 3-5 mm in diameter and 13-15 cm long. Thinner cuttings will root, but they don't develop into strong plants. Cut your propagation material with a sharp short-nosed shear or scissors. Clean you shear or scissors with alcohol before you begin. The cut at the base should be at a 45° angle. Place the cutting into a beaker or other vessel with clean water 7-8 cm deep.

Don't overcrowd the collection vessel. Bring the vessels filled with cuttings to the area where you will prepare the cuttings. Damage results from overcrowding the cuttings.

Prepare the seedling tray by wetting the growing media and allow excess water to drain off. May holes in each cell with a tool approximately 5 mm in diameter. Once the excess water has drained off the tray is ready to use. Place the tray on your left if you are right-handed and your other tools and supplies on your right.

Wash hands with soap and water.

Affix a new sterile scalpel blade onto the scalpel handle.

Clean the cutting board with alcohol.

Place a single cutting on the cutting board.

With a scalpel cut the leaves from the bottom up for 8-10 cm.

Chop the remaining leave to 50% of their size.

Dip the bottom 1-2 cm of the cutting into the rooting compound.

Insert the cutting into the hole made in a cell of the media in the seedling tray.

Once the seedling tray is full, place it in a closed rooting box.

Keep the seedling trays in a place with the temperature between 24-27°C and 16-18 hours of light.

Water once a day to a slight excess, which will maintain the high humidity inside the rooting box.

Figure 9. Shows how to prepare a cutting for rooting.

Your greenhouse helps to reduce insect infestations, only if you use it properly. Insects can enter the greenhouse when you come in or exit. That is why we designed the MPG with double door systems with positive pressure. When the outside door opens, it turns on the fan creating a barrier against insects coming inside. Don't leave the door open unnecessarily. Brush off your clothes before entering. Often, insects are on our clothes without our knowledge.

Lighting

Unless you are a qualified electrician, please don't set up your lighting system by yourself.

Equipment

1. Fuse box (water proof) if inside the

Greenhouse

a. main safety breaker
b. circuit breakers
c. neutral bus bar
d. grounding wire

1. Water proof wiring
2. Wire cutters
3. Wire connectors
4. Long nose plyers
5. Chains for hanging the

Light fixtures.

1. Light fixtures

A lumen is the amount of light emitted per second from any light source. There is an optimal amount of exposure to lumens which results in the healthy vigorous plant growth. Depending on plant density and variety, one needs between 3300 to 8800 lumens/m2.

PAR Light

Photosynthetically active radiation (PAR) describes the spectral range (wave band) of solar radiation from 400 to 700 nanometers. This is the range of radiation that photosynthetic organisms can convert light to chemical energy via the process of photosynthesis[1]. PAR parallels with the range of light[2] visible to the human eye.

Blue Light

The most important blue wavelengths are from 430 to 450 nm. This portion of the light spectrum is cool light. These wavelengths encourage vegetative growth through vigorous root growth and intense photosynthesis. Blue light is often used alone during the early phases of plant growth, such as starting seedling or maintaining mother plants, when flowering is undesirable.

Red Light

The longer wavelengths of light are red. The most important wavelengths in the red spectrum are from 640 to 680 nm. These wavelengths encourage stem growth, flowering, fruit production, and chlorophyll production. The red wavelengths are warm light and they are naturally more prevalent in sunlight during the shorter days of fall and winter.

Green and Yellow Light

Some of the green and yellow light reflects off the plant, giving the plant a green color. While most of the absorbed wavelengths are in the red and blue ranges, recent research shows that plants absorb some green and yellow light and use it in the photosynthesis process. A light source that provides light in the entire visible range will better meet the needs of the plant.

---

1. https://en.wikipedia.org/wiki/Photosynthesis

2. https://en.wikipedia.org/wiki/Light

Light Intensity

Sunlight provides far greater intensity than artificial lighting. Not all plants need the same light intensities. Some plants prefer the high intensity of full sun, while others prefer moderate sun or shade. In artificial lighting, the plant needs to be close to the light for highest light intensity.

Abundant Light:

The single most important factor for producing healthy Cannabis in a greenhouse is light. If you employ intense and profuse amounts of light will encourage plant growth and allow you to harvest often. Not only is the light you use crucial to the survival of your Cannabis, it will determine how quickly and sturdily your Cannabis will grow.

LEDs

Over the past ten years the lights used for greenhouse and indoor production have change to LEDs. They are cheaper to operate, and provide better growing (PAR) light. Photosynthetically Active Radiation (PAR) is the amount of light available for photosynthesis. This is light in the 400 to 700 nanometer wavelength range. PAR is subject to seasonal changes. It also varies depending on the latitude and time of day.

The advantages of employing LED lights are:

Quick Harvest Cycle. LED grow lights enable the grower to change the daylight hours and the amount of red wavelength light at the exact right time to maximize the plant growth rate.

Increased Lifespan

LED grow lights have a lifespan of over 50,000 hours, which is much longer than traditional lighting systems. This is because of the low operating temperature of the lights.

Traditional lighting systems produce large amounts of heat. This reduces the lifespans of the bulbs. The longer lifespan of LEDs reduces costs.

Energy Savings

LED grow lights are more efficient than conventional systems. LEDS consume 60% less energy to provide the same amount of light.

LED diode does not burn anything to produce light. Their reduced use of energy and heat production, lower energy bills.

Healthier Plants

LEDs emit more ultraviolet (UV) rays[1]. Infrared (IR) rays and heat reduce plant growth. Employing LED grow lights, limits heat and harmful

---

1. https://growlightinfo.com/the-effect-of-uv-light-on-plants/

wavelengths of light. This results in water and energy absorbed by the plant, which are used for growth and survival.

Target Wavelength

LED grow lights provide better regulation enable the grower to regulate the wavelengths of light, which means we can give plants the exact light they need for photosynthesis (the action spectrum[2]).

Traditional lighting systems emit a significant amount of light in the green and yellow wavelengths, which plants find little use. Plants need little green and yellow light. Excess green and yellow is wasted energy.

With LEDs, you can give the plants the exact spectrum of light they need to grow. No light goes to waste, and it's economical.

Full Spectrum

Advanced LED units emit a balanced full spectrum of light. As mentioned above, they give you all the light your plants need and no extraneous radiation.

Many companies produce units that allow you to turn off specific wavelengths, so they will emit the perfect light for the various stages of plant growth.

Cool Operating Temperature

LED grow lights produce lower amounts of heat. HID lighting systems generate very high temperatures. If they are too close to the plant, they can burn them. LED light has little effect on the operating temperature in a greenhouse.

Environment Friendly

LED grow lights are 100% recyclable. HID lights contain toxic substances like mercury.

Disadvantages of LED Grow Lights

Price The initial investment in LED lighting is more expensive than a traditional light sources.

---

2. https://growlightinfo.com/absorption-spectrum-vs-action-spectrum-differences-explained/

Directional light: LEDs are light flashlights, there light is directional. This reduces the area a unit of LED can provide light.

Temperature sensitivity–Quality of diodes: The efficiency of the diodes is directly correlated to his running temperature. The lower the temperature the more efficient the LED diodes are. Diodes that operate at high temperatures will burn out faster.

Electricity in the Greenhouse

Use of electricity to power lights and ventilation requires special care. You'll need to plan your grow-space so that electrical components — lights, plug-ins, wires, and ballasts — are off the ground and away from any water or damp areas. Water and electricity can make for dangerous conditions. Intricate growing systems which employ large amounts of electricity should be wired with their own fuse box or circuit breakers. If you're not completely competent at wiring and know the safety regulations, hire an electrician to help you with this. Electric safety is a primary consideration.

Light sources should be as close to your Cannabis as possible without burning them. You can test this by carefully putting the back of your hand at the top of your plants. If the heat is uncomfortably warm for your skin, it's too close.

Fertilizer Requirements

Fertilization has a major effect on the on the growth and production of secondary metabolites. The appropriate nutritional regime, i.e., organic fertilizers, supplements, and bio stimulants, is crucial to production of medical cannabis.

NPK stands for nitrogen, phosphorus and potassium. They call these three nutrients, macronutrients as the plant needs them in large amounts.

Nitrogen: Although air contains 78% nitrogen, most plants can't utilize it. They need to obtain the nitrogen via their roots from the soil. Nitrogen is important for the photosynthesis process. It is a key element in the diet of a cannabis plant during the vegetative stage.

Phosphorous: Plants have a hard time absorbing phosphorus from the soil because it becomes readily combined with other elements, which make it hard for the roots to absorb. Phosphorous is key for developing strong roots. Flowering plants need extra phosphorus for flowering and bud formation.

Potassium: Potassium strengthens a plant's metabolism. It is necessary for production of vital proteins and photosynthesis. Potassium strengthens the plant's immune system, making more resistant to infections, diseases, and pests.

Secondary macronutrients are sulfur, which is an important part of amino acids and therefore proteins. Calcium regulates transport of other nutrients into the plant. It also activates certain plant enzymes. Magnesium is the central atom in chlorophyll.

Micronutrients

Micronutrients, though in small amounts are still vitally important for good plant growth. Boron (B), Zinc (Zn), Silicon (Si), Copper (Cu), Manganese (Mn), Iron (Fe), Chloride (Cl) and Molybdenum (Mo) are used by the plant in minute amounts, but are as important to plant growth and development as the macronutrients. Some micronutrients control the uptake of major nutrients and key processes.

Boron is a vital element of cell wall formation and is key for the germination of pollen grains and growth of pollen tubes.

Zinc helps plant growth hormones and enzymatic activity. It is essential for chlorophyll production and carbohydrate formation.

Copper has an important role in photosynthesis. This element improves the flavor of fruits and vegetables.

Manganese assists in chlorophyll synthesis and increases the accessibility of phosphorus and calcium.

Iron helps the formation of chlorophyll and acts as an oxygen carrier.

Chloride promotes crop.

Molybdenum is needed to convert inorganic phosphates to organic forms in the plant and aids in the nodulation of legumes, especially in acidic soils.

Silicon reinforces the cell wall and increases both crop quality and yields.

Table 2 outlines the general total nitrogen needs of Cannabis during their growing season.

Table 2. General Nitrogen Needs of Greenhouse Grown Cannabis.

Age of Plant (rooted)	Total Nitrogen in ppm
0-2 weeks	30-100
3-4 weeks	125-200
5-6 weeks	200-389
7-8 weeks	389
9-11 weeks	283
12-16 weeks	283

Another general rule of preparing inorganic fertilizer. Mix one bag of 25 kg of fertilizer with 100 liters of water to be your stock solution. Full grown plant needs 2% of this stock solution injected into the water system.

In the paper by Caplan et al. 2017 they also found that increased fertilizer rate led to increased growth and yield but reduced levels of THC, THCA, and CBGA.

In a recent paper Bernstein et al. 2019 conducted research on the effects of fertilizer on the secondary metabolites of Cannabis. Their study evaluated the effects of nutritional supplementations, humic acids (HAs) and inorganic N, P, and K, to affect the cannabinoid profile throughout the various parts of the plant. Bernstein's team gave three nutrient treatments, compared to a commercial control treatment. The three nutrition treatments with the addition of HA, increased phosphate, or enhanced NPK.

Their results showed cannabinoids metabolism sensitivity to mineral nutrition. The nutritional supplements altered cannabinoid levels. The changes turned out to be location and organ specific. This also altered between the cannabinoids examined. Increased levels of P didn't affect THC, CBD, CBN, and CBG concentrations in the flowers from the top of the plants. They observed a 16 percent reduction of THC concentration in the inflorescence leaves. Increased levels of NPK and HA also caused organ-specific and spatially specific reactions in the plant. NPK significantly increased CBG levels in flowers and lowered CBN levels in both flowers and inflorescence leaves.

The results with humic acid showed it reduced the natural spatial variability of the cannabinoids studied. However, the increased uniformity reduced levels of cannabinoids at the upper part of the plants. Humic acid caused a significant reduction of THC and CBD.

"The results confirm the potential of environmental factors to regulate concentrations of individual cannabinoids in medical cannabis."

Organic Fertilizers

Manure is the feces of farm animals such as a cow, sheep, poultry and horses. This fertilizer is normally composited and allowed to break down. The chemical composition of the manure depends on what the animal is feed and how they store the manure.

Manure is a by-product of livestock production and an excellent source of nutrients for plant growth. Dung contains nitrogen (N), phosphorus (P), potassium (K) and micronutrients. Manure contains organic matter that improves soil tilth, aeration and water holding capacity.

Advantages of Organic Fertilizers

They release nutrients, as they break down.

They improve the structure of the soil and increase its ability to hold water and nutrients.

Since they are slow-release fertilizers, it's very difficult to over fertilize the plants.

Little to no risk of harmful buildups of chemicals and salts.

They are renewable, biodegradable, sustainable, and non-harmful to the environment.

Table 3 Chemical Composition of Animal Manures.

TABLE 3: Typical Manure Characteristics

	Dairy Cow	Beef Cow	Chicken	Hog
Dry Matter Content (%)				
Solid	26	23	55	9
Liquid (fresh, diluted)	7	8	17	6
Total Nutrient Content (Approximate)				
Nitrogen				
pounds/ton	10	14	25	10
pounds/1,000 gallons	25	39	70	28
Phosphate, as P2O5				
pounds/ton	6	9	25	6
pounds/1,000 gallons	9	25	70	9
Potash, as K20				
pounds/ton	7	11	12	9
pounds/1,000 gallons	20	31	33	34
solid manure (tons)	10	7	4	10
liquid manure (gallons)	4000	2500	1500	3600

The values given in the above table need to be viewed with caution. This is because of the chemical composition of manures from even the same type of animal will fluctuate significantly from one farm to another. The chemical composition differs because of the various feeds, mineral supplements, bedding materials, and storage systems. On a given farm if feeding, bedding, and storage practices remain relatively similar, the manure nutrient characteristics will tend to be constant from year to year. Differences in yearly rainfall can affect stored manure by making it more or less diluted.

Manure is a "complete" fertilizer; it has a high percentage of organic matter, but little nutrients. Manures are most valuable as organic soil amendments[1] and mulches. Fresh manure as a fertilizer can burn plants.

---

1. https://www.planetnatural.com/product-category/organic-gardening/soil-care/soil-amendments/

Blood meal is dried powdered blood collected from cattle slaughterhouses. It's a rich source of nitrogen. Take care not to give excess amounts, as it will burn the roots. Apply blood meal[2] before planting to stimulate leaf growth.

Bone meal is finely ground bone. Another by-product from animal slaughterhouses. An excellent source of calcium and has up to 15% phosphate. Bone meal[3] promotes strong root systems and flowering. Add when the blooming stage begins.

Bat guano is rich in soluble nitrogen, phosphorous and trace elements. They usually sell it as a powder. Bat guano may be used any time of the year as a top dressing or diluted and used as a foliar spray.

It is most effectively used at the root zone to heighten flower and root development. Amend your soil, use as a top dressing or create an "organic tea" and apply directly to plant roots. Eco-friendly harvesting from centuries-old cave deposits.

They gather South American seabird guano off the rocks of arid Sea Islands. There is little rainfall and decomposition is minimal. This results in a high percentage of nitrogen, phosphorous and other nutrients.

One differentiates between red and white seabird guano by age and origin. Red Guan is fossilized guano. It is a biogenic sediment. It is pure phosphate fertilizer with 20–30% phosphoric acid content (P2O5). Differences are dependent of source. White Guano represents a recent formation. This guano is daily animal excrements—especially by seabirds. It comprises a 10–12% nitrogen, 10–12% phosphoric acid (P2O5) and 3% potash (K2O). Once again, the differences in percentages depends on the source.

Shellfish fertilizer or shell meal is from crushed bones or shells of shellfish. One analysis showed that shell meal contains 36.4% calcium, 0.002% iron, 0.097% potassium, 0.398% magnesium, 0.152% sodium, 0.091% sulfur, and 0.116% phosphorus. Crab shells contain high levels of chitin. The high levels of chitin provide a perfect feeding ground for chitin eating bacteria; increasing their

---

2. https://www.planetnatural.com/product/blood-meal-50-lb/

3. https://www.planetnatural.com/product/bone-meal-50-lb/

population in the soil. These bacteria feed on the chitin in the cell walls of nematodes and fungi in the soil.

Rock phosphate is a calcium phosphate rock that is ground to tiny pellets. This rock contains over 30% phosphate and many trace elements. Rock phosphate[4] does not leach out of the soil. It remains unchanged until taken up by the roots.

Greensand is an iron potassium silicate which gives the mineral a green tint. Greensand[5] is rich in iron, potassium and numerous micronutrients.

Fish emulsion is finely pulverized fish partially decomposed. It has a strong fishy smell. Like blood meal, fish emulsion should be used carefully to prevent burning plant roots.

Calculating Nitrogen content of manure.

Basis for Manure application rates:

Soil Analyzes

Fertilizer Recommendations,

Manure Analyzes

Timing

Method of Application

Weather Conditions.

Manure application rates have been based on nitrogen needs to achieve the target yield.

Not all the nitrogen in the manure is available to the crop in the first year after application. This results in estimating the available N in the manure. The results of the manure test provide results for total N and ammonium N of that lot of manure. Each lot is different and one can't extrapolate to another lot of

---

4. https://www.planetnatural.com/product/rock-phosphate-50-lb/

5. https://www.planetnatural.com/product/greensand-50-lb/

manure accurately. Calculate organic N as the difference between total N and ammonium N.

Organic N = Total N–Ammonium N

One needs to estimate both the inorganic (ammonium) and organic forms to get the total available nitrogen. Ammonium is 100% available to the plants, but susceptible to losses by volatilization into ammonia gas.

Available Ammonium N = Total Ammonium N x (100%–% Volatilization Loss).

One must mineralize organic nitrogen before it is available to the plant. The proportion of organic N in manure available to the following crop is around twenty-five percent:

Available Organic N = 25% Organic N

Therefore, Total available nitrogen from manure is: Total Available N = (Ammonium N–Volatilization loss) + 25% Organic N

Disadvantages of Organic Fertilizer:

- Microorganisms are needed to decompose the fertilizer, which causes the release nutrients into the soil. The microorganisms need a warmth and moisture environment to be effective. This makes organic fertilizer's effectiveness is seasonally limited.
- Organic fertilizers break down according to the microclimate in which they are situated. They don't release nutrients when you need them. Patience is required. Plants don't react immediately after application. Short-term results can actually result in mineral deficiencies during the first months after application.
- Nutrient ratios are often unknown, and the overall percentage is lower than chemical fertilizers. This is a critical factor if you want to produce medical Cannabis with repeatable results.

Table 4. Summation of Growing Conditions

This table is for rooted cuttings

Week	EC	RH	CO2 ppm	Lumen /per m2 Light Intensity	nm Wavelength	temperature
1	[illegible]	[illegible]	[illegible]	[illegible]	[illegible]	[illegible]
2	1.0-2.0	65-75	700	50,000	380-500	24-30 C
3	1.0-2.0	65-75	700	55,000	380-500	24-30 C
4	1.0-2.0	65-75	700	60,000	380-500	24-30 C
5	1.0-2.0	65-75	800	70,000	380-500	24-30 C
6	1.0-2.0	65-75	800	70,000	380-500	24-30 C
7	1.0-2.0	65-75	800	70,000	380-500	24-30 C
8	1.0-2.0	65-75	800	70,000	380-500	24-30 C
9	1.0-2.0	65-75	1200	100,000	635-700	24-30 C
10	1.0-2.0	65-75	1200	100,000	635-700	24-30 C
11	1.0-2.0	65-75	1200	100,000	635-700	24-30 C
12	1.0-2.0	65-75	1200	100,000	635-700	24-30 C
13	1.0-2.0	65-75	1200	100,000	635-700	24-30 C
14	1.0-2.0	65-75	1200	100,000	635-700	24-30 C
15	1.0-2.0	65-75	1200	100,000	635-700	24-30 C
16	1.0-2.0	65-75	1200	100,000	635-700	24-30 C

Week	ppm	ppm	ppm	ppm	ppm	ppm
1	N	P	K	pH	Ca	Mg
2	25	100	300	5.8-6.5	200	25
3	50	125	300	5.8-6.5	200	25
4	50	150	300	5.8-6.5	200	25
5	75	175	300	5.8-6.5	200	25
6	75	200	300	5.8-6.5	200	25
7	100	125	300	5.8-6.5	100	25
8	100	300	300	5.8-6.5	250	25
9	125	300	250	5.8-6.5	250	50
10	150	300	250	5.8-6.5	250	50
11	180	300	400	5.8-6.5	200	50
12	180	300	400	5.8-6.5	200	25
13	220	300	400	5.8-6.5	300	25
14	220	300	400	5.8-6.5	300	25
15	240	600	600	5.8-6.5	300	20
16	240	600	600	5.8-6.5	300	20

Renewal of Plants

The Mini Professional Greenhouse is an excellent location for growing your Cannabis all year long. After harvest, one can renew the Cannabis plants for another season. Yields are less, but this is offset by a shorter season. A renewed Cannabis plant can reduce your vegetative stage by 2-4 weeks.

The key to renewing a Cannabis plant is not to remove all the leaves and branches during harvest. Plant renewal is based on the large root system developed during the previous season. It takes 7-10 days for a severely pruned plant to initiate new stems and leaves. If the plants are healthy, it is possible to save 3-4 weeks of the vegetative stage to your next crop. Yields are normally less, but if grown well it evens out.

Growth Media

Selecting of your growth media is of utmost importance. It influences how much fertilizer you give and your irrigation regime. Media like volcanic rock need more frequent irrigations than peat moss, which can absorb water and release it.

The characteristics of a good potting mix are:

Well-drained, an air-filled porosity of at least 15%

Re-wets easily

Doesn't shrink away from the side of the pot as it dries

Optimum weight–not too heavy to lift, not so light as to blow over easily

Suitable pH, between 5.0 and 6.8 is satisfactory for most plants

Sterilized without producing harmful by-products

Stored without significant changes in physical or chemical properties

Readily available

Not expensive.

Table 4. Characteristics of Growing Media.

Substrate	Bulk density	Water retention	Porosity	Cation exchange capacity
Sawdust	Low	High	Medium	High
Rice hulls	Low	Low	High	Medium
Vermiculite	Low	High	Medium	High
Peat moss	Low	High	High	High
Bark	Low	Medium	Medium	Medium
Coconut / Coir Dust	Low	High	High	Medium
Sand	High	Low	Medium	Low
Units	(g/cm3)	%	%	(meq/100g)
Low:	0,25	20	5	10
Medium	0,25 - 0,75	20-60	5-30	10-100
High:	0,75	60	30	100

Caplan et al. 2017 found very significant differences between low and higher container capacity coco peat (coir). The container capacity is defined as the water-holding capacity. It signifies the maximum amount of water held by a plant's growth medium within a container before gravity forces the water to flow out of the container's drainage holes. Caplan found that the higher container capacity coco peat gave significantly better results.

Growing Methods

Many growing systems are used to grow Cannabis. Some of them excellent, but not compatible for smaller Agro4pro greenhouses. This is in reference to the floating raft system used to grow herbs and lettuce. The moving float system is an excellent system but needs more space.

Traditional Organic Production

In most countries organic crops must be connected to the soil. Recent studies have shown that Cannabis like cilantro (Karadjov, 2019) removes heavy metals from the soil. Most nations don't require soil or water testing for organic growing.

The other problem with organic growing is the resulting extracts. The effects of nutrients and environmental conditions greatly affect production of secondary metabolites in plants. Scientists have isolated 113 different Cannabinoids in Cannabis. They have identified over a hundred and forty terpenes in Cannabis. Only a minority of them have scientists characterized for their medicinal function.

The aim of the medical Cannabis industry is to compete with the gigantic pharmaceutical industry. To accomplish this, the industry needs repeatability. As mentioned above, the composition of the organic fertilizers is not uniform. Therefore, using the same conditions and the same brand of organic fertilizer will give you a different terpene and cannabinoid chemical profile.

The pharmaceutical industry based its foundation on the concept of finding the most active ingredient, isolating it and turning it into a pill. Cannabis companies attempted to follow this concept and found that their products were not as effective as whole plant extracts. The reason is the interactions (both synergetic and antagonistic) between the various cannabinoids and terpenes. It will take years of research to clarify the multiple reactions. In the meantime, by maintaining close control over the nutrients and environmental conditions one can improve the uniformity of his extracts.

Organic production in the soil.

Though not required by organic standards, have your soil examined by a qualified laboratory for nematodes, heavy metals and pesticide residues. Another method of eliminating Nematodes control is adding compost to your soil every year over a five-year period.

There are several variations in growing in the soil. All these variations require 18 hours of light during vegetative stage and 12 hours of light during the blooming stage. A blackout system is available with your MPG.

Tools and Equipment for growing in the soil.

1. Pitchfork for turning soil.
2. Rack
3. Hole maker.
4. Hoe to remove weeds.
5. 1 kg hammer.
6. Wooden or metal stakes for.
7. Trellising
8. Synthetic twine or plastic netting for trellising.
9. Pruning shears.
10. Plastic boxes for harvesting (preferably perforated.

Preparation of Soil.

If you are going to add compost or manure to the soil, this is the time.

a. Spread the compost or manure evenly over the soil surface.
b. Use a pitchfork turn the soil and mix in the compost.
c. Rack the soil to create an even surface.

The traditional method is one plant per meter squared.

1. Lay out your irrigation system. Make sure your dripper is 4-6 cm away from the stem. Place the dripper line in the middle of your row. Drippers should be 1 meter apart. The row should be 1 meter wide and the aisle in between rows should be 80 cm to allow you to pass through and care for the plants when they are larger.
2. Transplant your rooted cuttings. First use a pointed stick or tool to make the holes. Then place a rooted cutting in the hole. Firm the soil around the roots so there is good contact between the roots and the soil. Air pockets can stop the flow of water and damage the plants.

3. During the vegetative stage provide more blue light.
4. Set up your support system when the plants are 20-25 cm tall.
5. Check the EC and pH of your nutrient solution twice a week. Once every two weeks take a soil sample from next to the roots of one of your plants. Add cooled boiled water until excess water drips from the sample. Collect the excess and analyze it for EC and pH.
6. Increase the amount of water and fertilizer as your plants grow. When you switch to a 12-hour day, reduce the nitrogen in your fertilizer.
7. Change your lights to more dominantly red light.
8. Once the plants flower, be diligent to remove any male flowers that might appear.
9. Use latex gloves to harvest flowers as the resin will get on your hands.

This method can produce a huge plant with high yields, if grown properly. Research on uniformity of oil production has shown that on large plants the variation between flowers can be very large.

The second method is to plant four to eight plants per meter squared. Plants are smaller, but if grown well you should be able to equal the same yield as one large plant. The advantages are more uniform oil production and shorter plants that are easier to care for during the season. The disadvantage is you need many more plantlets. You also need more water emitters for your larger plant population.

The third method is Sea of Green (SOG). Plant density for SOG is between fifteen to thirty plants per square meter. Plants are very short, yields are small, but multiplied by the number of plants you should get a yield equal to a single large plant. The advantages are like the second method but even more pronounced. Equally the disadvantage of an even large number of plantlets needed.

Supports

Cannabis grows quickly and needs support, or it will flop over and break its branches.

There are several methods of supporting the plants. All the systems require structural support to anchor your support system.

Figure 10. Plastic Net Support for Cannabis Plants.

The figure shows a plastic trellis netting place over the young Cannabis plants. The pots have a 25 cm diameter which works out to have sixteen plants per square meter. In this photo the hoops of the screen house support the trellis netting. Your upright posts of the MPG can be used as the support anchors for your trellising system.

The first trellis net support should be in place while the plants are still small, as shown in the figure above. The second support should be 30-40 cm above the first. To avoid large amounts of hand labor, have the second support trellis in place after one week. Then as the plant grow lift it once or twice until the netting is at the correct height.

Another method of support is steel cables strung above your plants at a height of 2.00 to 2.20 meters. Attach strings to the support cables. One for every plant like growing indeterminate tomatoes.

Weekly Checklist

Table 5. Weekly Plant Care Checklist.

Action	Daily	Once/ week	Twice/ week	Three times/week
Water leaks & clogs			X	
Water Filter		X		
Structure		X		
Examine Emitters		X		
EC				X
Plant Health	X			
Soil Moisture	X			
pH				X
Insects			X	
Diseases			X	
Fertilizer Tank	X			
Trellising			X	
Sanitation	X			
Pruning		X		
Fans		X		
Electric system		X		

Water leaks and clogs-check from the source of your water along your line through the head and onto the emitters. Calcium deposits cause most clogs in the water system. Clean emitters by adding acid to the water.

Calculation Method: The injection rate of the acid to the treated zone can be figured in the following way: (FLOW IN LPM) X.36 = INJECTION RATE IN L.P.H. For example: Flow = 378 l.p.m. 378 x 0.36= 136 l.p.h. What amount of acid (in gallons) is required? Since the acid should be injected for only fifteen minutes, the total gallons of acid to be used will always be a fourth of the injection rate. For example: 136/4 = 34 liters.

Cleaning water filters.

Close the water to the irrigation system.

Remove the cover holding the mesh filter in the housing by turning it counterclockwise.

Lift the filter out of the housing. Clean the filter with a small brush (i.e., toothbrush) removing any sediment. Use clean water to loosen and remove any debris that remains. If you prefer, rinse the filter with a hose.

Open the ends of your irrigation lines. Then turn on water and allow it to run through the irrigation system without the filters in place, to clean out the lines. Any debris, mud, and sand will come out the end of your irrigation line. When the water turns clean close off the end.

Turn off the water and replace the filter. Turn the water on.

Examine the structure for holes or tears in the materials covering the greenhouse. Treat any signs of rust.

Walk along your rows of plants, checking that each emitter works properly. If not, bang the emitter several times to see if it will work. If not, the emitters are probably clogged calcium sediment. Treat with dilute acid to clean them.

Check the Electric Conductivity (EC) of the water coming out of your growing vessel. EC measures the amount of salts (fertilizer) in the water. If the EC is high cut back on the amount of fertilizer, you are giving. Cannabis is fairly tolerant to high EC. It is best to keep the EC between 1.5 to 2.5. Make sure you calibrate your EC meter before taking a reading every time.

Examine the foliage of your plants every day. Above is the chart showing nutrient excesses and deficiencies. Also look of signs of insect or disease infestation.

Monitor soil moisture with a tensiometer or by feeling the growing media in your fingers. If dry make sure the emitters are working.

Best pH to grow Cannabis is 5.5 to 6.1. Make sure you calibrate your pH meter before taking a reading every time.

Using a magnifying glass, check a sample of the under leaves for any insects. Don't delay treatment.

Learn how to identify the various insects that infest Cannabis plants.

Learn how to identify the various diseases that infest Cannabis plants.

Check your fertilizer tank to make sure it's closed and nothing from the outside can get in to contaminate your fertilizer concentration. Check to see if you have sufficient reserves and the vessel itself has no holes or damage.

Trellising is a means of supporting your plants. Cannabis is fast growing and without support will flop over and break. If you are using netting, make sure the netting is in place long before you need it. Let the plants grow through the netting, to avoid lots of excess hand labor.

Sanitation. Cleanliness is next to Godliness. Remove all dead and trimmed plant material to a place outside the greenhouse. Let it dry and then incinerated it. It is very difficult to compost Cannabis because of the very strong fibers in the stems. Clean tools outside of the greenhouse.

The objective of pruning is to force the growth of the plant into the shape that you desire. Female plants can produce male flowers. Often male flowers form on the bottom third of the plant. Keep the bottom quarter clean so you can easily identify male flowers.

The fans have an important role in the greenhouse. They in the entrance provides positive pressure to keep insects out of the greenhouse. The other fans circulate the air by one of them bringing air into the greenhouse and the other acting as an exhaust fan pulling air out. The fans should exchange the entire amount of air at a rate of 30-60 times an hour.

Calculating the CFM for your Greenhouse

You can determine air exchange by the CFM, or cubic feet per minute of your fans. It measures how much air the fan moves in a measured time frame. Calculating CFM's is done by determining the amount of air in the greenhouse. Multiply length by width by the height to get the total air volume.

Example: Your greenhouse is 6m wide, 4m long and 4.5m high. The volume would be 6x4x4.5=108 m3. 108 m3, which is equal to 3814 cubic feet.

If you want to exchange the air 40 times an hour then 40 x 3814 ft3=152,560 ft3. Divide 152,560 by 60 minutes = 2,542CFM. You will need an 18-inch fan to move that much air.

Electrical system. Make sure that any electrics in the greenhouse are waterproof. No wires should run in places where people can step on or trip on them.

Growing in vessels with artificial media.

New artificial media is completely sterile and free of all toxins and heavy metals. The most popular growing vessels are plastic pots, plastic grow bags without media, grow bags with a variety of artificial media and rock wool. Ceramics are fine but expensive and heavy to move.

There are biodegradable pots available made from recycled paper. Biodegradable plastics growing pots are now available.

Hydroponics

They define hydroponics as growing plants in sand, gravel, or liquid, with added nutrients but without soil. You can buy hydroponic systems from stores that sell hydroponic equipment and systems or you can build the system yourself.

There are six types of Hydroponics:

Wick Systems

Deep Water Culture

Drip Systems

Ebb and Flow (Flood and Drain)

Nutrient Film Technique

Aeroponics

See Figure11. Below for an efficient method of planning the layout of your Mini Professional Greenhouse (MPG).

Figure 11. Efficient Layout for MPG.

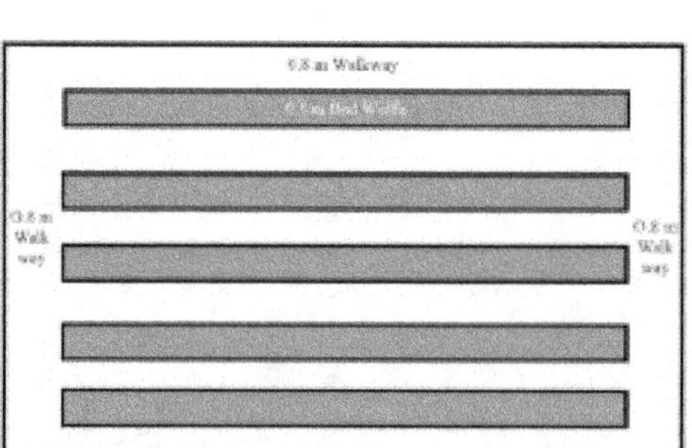

The advantages of hydroponics are:

Plants grow faster.

Plants can be grown all year long.

Higher yields per season.

Hydroponics systems use 90% less water.

No negative environmental impact from water

run-off.

Reduced fungal, soil-borne diseases, or pests. Hence, there's little or no need for pesticides.

It requires less labor compared to traditional farming.

Disadvantages of Hydroponics

Initial investment is more expensive.

Although there is less labor involved, managing this system requires diligence and daily monitoring.

If nutrients, oxygen or water is interrupted, the plants suffer and die quickly.

Basic equipment for hydroponic systems.

Air Pump

Air Stone

Vessel for Nutrient Solution Reservoir.

Vessel to hold growing media

Mesh Pots

Nutrient Solution pump

Another consideration: will you grow your Cannabis in soil or use hydroponics (growing without soil)? Farmers and customers have long believed that vegetables and Cannabis grown in soil will naturally taste better. With the advent of advanced hydroponics-nutrient solutions, that belief is changing. Different commercial and/ or homemade hydroponics systems make it easy to introduce nutrients to your plants and a wide array of nutrient solutions will ensure your Cannabis get everything they would from soil. Again, your indoor-gardening supplier is your best source of information regarding which hydroponics nutrient solutions to use.

We recommend beginners to grow directly in soil. Before growing your first crop for use, grow cannabis or cilantro on the soil to remove any heavy metals that might be there. After harvest, dry the plants and burn them in a safe place.

Those with outdoor gardening experience can easily translate that knowledge to growing indoors. With good drainage, proper soil and nutrients and a minimum of attention, raising Cannabis in soil is easy. Cannabis don't require extensive fertilizing. In fact, over fertilizing your Cannabis plants will mean more vegetative growth and a larger plant. The larger the plant the less uniform the oil content is among the various flowers. Mediterranean conditions — dry cool conditions with less abundant nutrients and a near neutral or slightly acidic pH level between 6 and 7 — will give smaller plants with more uniform oil content among the flowers.

Raising plants in soil can be less expensive for those without high-yield expectations. Soil is also more forgiving than hydroponics. Miss a watering or otherwise make a mistake and your plants will probably survive. Mistakes or oversights in hydroponics gardening can have faster and more severe consequences.

Modern hydroponics systems take away most of the room for error. And when done correctly, growing hydroponically can give quicker and greater yields. There are a number of ways to make your own hydroponics systems[1]. Even the simplest systems are complicated. The most sophisticated homemade systems

---

1. https://www.youtube.com/watch?v=DBME3l29G6Q&feature=related

may be beyond the capabilities of the home hobbyist and nearly as expensive to set-up compared to kits available from gardening supply stores.

Commercial hydroponics systems now come in a wide variety of methods and sizes. Wick systems, which use capillary action, are the simplest. Auto pots use a mechanical float valve that initiates watering when the growing medium goes dry. Ebb and flow systems flood the growing medium and allow it to drain. This pulls oxygen down to the root systems. Deep water culture systems use air pumps and air stones to keep water moving through clay stones or various gravel.

Figure 12. Wick Hydroponics.

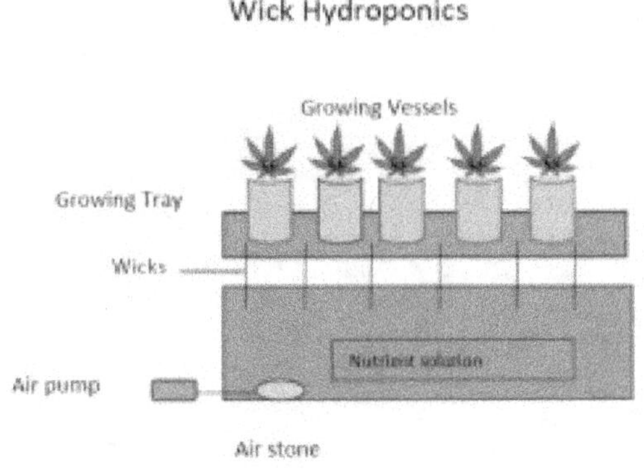

How to choose the right growing medium — coconut peat[2], soil conditioners[3], soilless mixes[4] — is a matter of preference and convenience. Many growers prefer Coco peat, because of its ability to wick air and moisture to your plants' roots. It's also compostable. Don't overlook ventilation and temperature in your greenhouse. Cannabis thrives in cooler temperatures than you might expect. Keeping your Cannabis in ideal temperatures 24-32oC degrees — can be difficult if using heat-producing grow lights. Using fans or other ventilation[5]

---

2. https://www.planetnatural.com/product-category/growing-indoors/growing-media/coconut-coir/

3. https://www.planetnatural.com/product-category/growing-indoors/growing-media/soil-conditioners/

4. https://www.planetnatural.com/product-category/growing-indoors/growing-media/soilless/

to control heat will also refresh the air which your Cannabis need for growth. Proper air-exchange will prevent this.

Deep Water Hydroponics

Deep water culture hydroponics is a method of growing plants in which the roots grow in an oxygenated nutrient solution, instead of in soil. The two best way to employ this method is to make ponds by digging down 60 cm or place them on bench supports 40-50 cm tall. One may use PVC or LLDPE plastic.

If you choose to use ponds, then make sure whatever support system you employ (wood, metal, cement), that there are no rough or pointy spots that could damage the pond liner. If you are using benches, you can also use plastic tubs. This plastic tubs come in various sizes.

Figure 13. Deep Water Hydroponics.

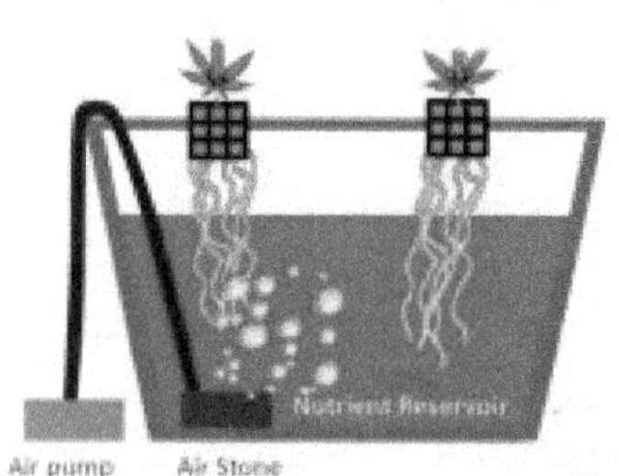

Advantages of Deep-Water Culture Systems

Deep water culture systems are a good way to get started with hydroponics. It is more complicated from wick systems, yet simple enough for anyone to use. They often use this system with an increased number of plants/meters squared. The primary advantages of deep-water culture systems are:

Simple to setup. Deep water culture systems are easy to set up. They require a limited number of parts, which are simple to put together in a short time. The air pump is the only moving part and easy to configure.

---

5. https://www.planetnatural.com/product-category/growing-indoors/grow-rooms/fans-ducting/

Monitoring is fairly simple, but at least twice a day. Maintenance costs are very little once the system is set up.

Plants grow faster. This leads to larger plants with greater yields compared to soil-based cultivation.

Shortens the growth cycle, providing more crops over the same time frame.

Disadvantages

Fluctuations in pH and nutrient concentration. In small-scale systems, fast-growing plants cause rapid changes in the pH and concentration of the nutrient solution. These have to be monitored often to avoid problems of nutrient deficiencies in your plants.

Adjusting EC and pH is more difficult. Small systems with small volumes of nutrient solution, are more difficult to accurately adjust the pH and EC.

The temperature of small volumes of what are more difficult to keep within the target range. The ambient temperature of the growing space speedily alters the nutrient solution temperature.

One must maintain constant aeration of the water in a deep-water culture system. Plant roots will not survive sitting in water depleted of oxygen; they will die. Air pumps aren't expensive so always keep a spare on hand if your pump stops working.

Ebb and Flow

Ebb and Flow is simple, reliable, and has a low initial investment cost. Fill the pots with an inert medium, like perlite or vermiculite, which don't act like soil or provide nutrition to the plants. The media acts as an anchor for the roots and functions as a short-term reserve of nutrient solution. Your nutrient solution alternately floods the system and then ebbs (drains) away.

The growing bed must be water proof. One can fill the bed with media and plant directly or use artificial media in growing vessels. The bed is intermittently flooded for 5 to 10 minutes with a nutrient solution pumped from a supply tank. They place the nutrient solution reserve tank below the growing bed. This way the nutrient solution can drain back by gravity.

In commercial greenhouses they incorporate moving benches into the system. The benches move across the greenhouse on rails. You time the movement of the benches so that by the time the plants reach the other side; the crop is ready for harvest.

The disadvantage of the ebb and flow system is the necessity of filtering the nutrient solution in between uses and sterilized before use in another cycle. The method is inefficient in its use of water and plant nutrient reagents.

Follow the greenhouse plan above to create your ponds or benches. Beds should be 70-80 cm high off the ground with a lip of another 5 cm.

Figure 12. Ebb and Flow Hydroponics.

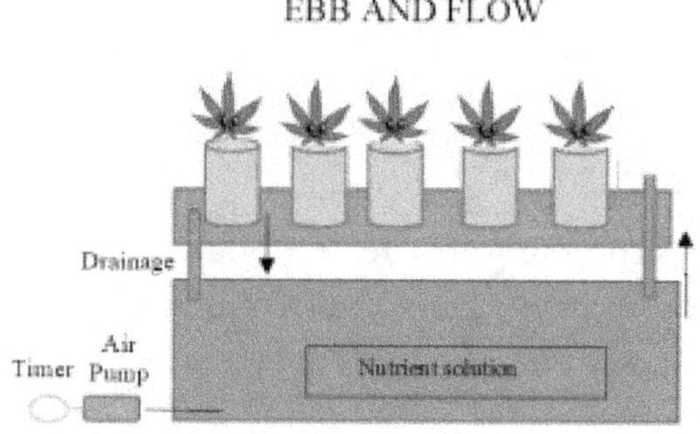

Nutrient Film Technique

They base nutrient Film Technique system on the right channel slope, flow rate, and channel length. The plant roots need exposure to suitable amounts of water, oxygen and nutrients. A shallow stream of nutrient solution should constantly circulate past the bare roots of plants in a watertight tunnel, also known as channels.

Gradient

The angle of the gradient of the trough is important to the way the nutrient solution flows through the system. A crucial factor is the solution shouldn't pool or gather around the roots. Stagnate water will cause root rot and defeat the benefits of this system.

During construction of the system, using a level and measuring the difference in height of the channel over a distance. A gradient is equal to the change in height over the length measured. A difference in 1 cm height over a meter length gives you a 1% slope. This is done by placing the channels in a framework with a build in gradient or on benches with something under the channels to create a difference in height.

It is difficult to build a channel that does not allow the solution to pool. Drain fittings, channel joints and even imperfections and depressions in the channel's surface can cause fluid to puddle. A shallow gradient (1:100–1%) is best. Practically, it works out to a 2.5-3.33% slope.

Flow Rate

The availability of nutrients to the plants depends on the nutrient solution flow rate. With the gradient, the two factors dictate the depth of nutrient solution at the bottom of the channel. This is the key to the success of the system;

If the film is too deep and you defeat the fundamental concept of the system. If the film is too thin, there won't be sufficient nutrients available to the plants. Flow rate results from the gradient and the pump speed.

Aim at a rate of 1 liter per minute. New young plants will need 500 ml per minute. Large adult plants should receive a flow rate of 2 liters per minute. Flow rates outside of these parameters can cause nutrient uptake issues.

Length of Channel

Some systems use nutrient oxygenation to further boost the oxygen available to the root system. An air stone in the reservoir or by allowing the solution to 'fall' back into the reservoir during its recirculation will provide aeration;

The length of the channels you use has an important effect on the oxygen levels of your nutrient solution. If the channel is too long, the oxygen content of the solution will become depleted by the time it reaches the end of its run;

The actual maximum length of the channel you use will obviously depend on factors such as your flow rate, gradient and number of plants. Don't exceed 10-meter lengths of channel. Longer channels for commercial set-ups are possible if you place multiple nutrient feeds, injecting your nutrient solution into the channel, at intervals along the length of it. Flow rates need adjusting. The minimum and maximum 2 liters/min.

They use narrow thin channels for growing leafy vegetables. Cannabis, being a larger plant, needs a wider channel. Because of the eventual size of channel, you need your cuttings prepared differently. Instead of using a standard seedling tray, use a deeper tray so you can get longer roots. Use cells that are 8-12 cm deep.

A suitable material for your channels is PVC sewage pipes. Four-inch pipes should be the minimum diameter. Six- and eight-inch pipes will support larger plants. Use an auger drill bit to drill out 8-10 cm holes every 50 cm. There is special mesh growing pots for hydroponics. These pots allow the roots to grow through them to reach the nutrient film. Close the ends of pipes with a rubber gasket and plastic cap.

Below Figure 13 shows a setup of NFT configured for the Sea of Green, high density planting.

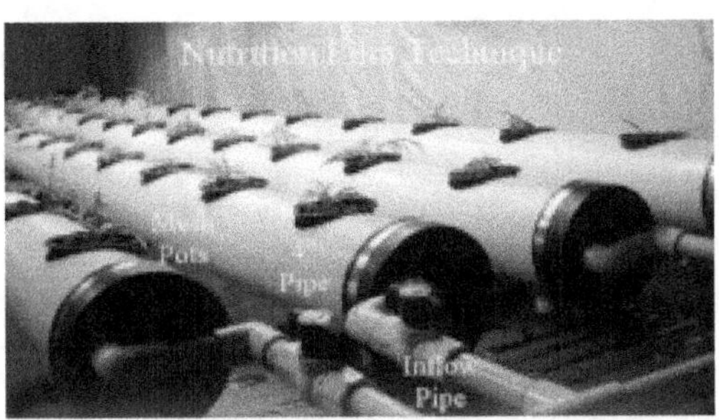
Nutrient Film Technique
Pots
2"
Pipe
Inflow
Pipe

Aeroponics

Aeroponics is growing plants[1] in an air[2] or mist[3] environment without the use of soil[4] or an aggregate[5] medium.

Aeroponics systems suspend the plant roots in the air, giving them with maximum exposure to oxygen. Plants absorb carbon dioxide from the air through their stomata as part of the process of photosynthesis. Roots need oxygen to aid in the absorption of the nutrients that are used to build new structures and grow. Thus, if you provide the best radiation to the upper part of your plant and maximize oxygen to your roots, the result will be best rate of growth possible.

Fig.14   Aeroponics   system

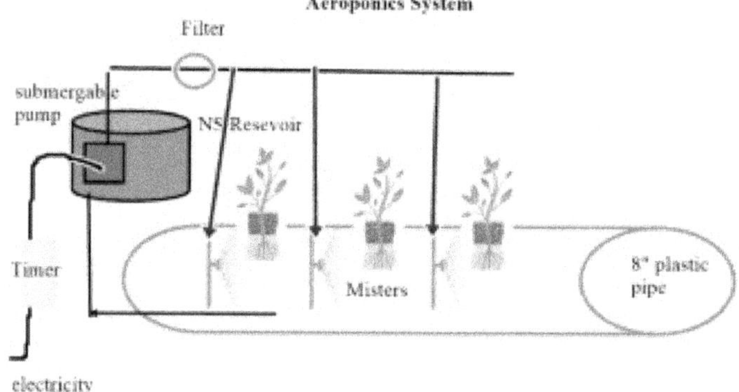

Equipment needed:

1. Electricity Source
2. Nutrient Solution Reservoir

1. https://en.wikipedia.org/wiki/Plants

2. https://en.wikipedia.org/wiki/Air

3. https://en.wikipedia.org/wiki/Mist

4. https://en.wikipedia.org/wiki/Soil

5. https://en.wikipedia.org/wiki/Construction_aggregate

3. Filter
4. Timer
5. Submergible Pump
6. 16mm Irrigation Hose
7. 8 Mm Irrigation Hose
8. 8mm Barb Connectors
9. Mist emitters 40-50 L/hr
10. 8" Plastic Pipe
11. Mesh Pots
12. Sterile Growth Media

Fig. 15 Root Growth in Aeroponics

Advantages of Aeroponics

Speedy growth: Plants grow quickly because their roots have access to high levels of oxygen 24/7.

Easy system maintenance- Regularly disinfect the root chamber, the reservoir and irrigation channels. The constant semi-moist environment of the root chamber perfect conditions for bacteria.

Nutrient absorption rate is higher; therefore, you need less need for nutrients and water.

Mobility–You can move plants moved without little effort.

Requires little space. They can in stacked growing chambers up one on top of each other. Aeroponics is modular, perfect for maximum efficiency.

Disadvantages of Aeroponics

Dependence on a perfectly working system. Aeroponics comprises high pressure pumps, sprinklers and timers. Trouble with any of them cause damage or death.

Technical knowledge required–One needs technical knowledge to run an aeroponics system. Correct amounts of nutrients are essential to achieve good yields.

Regular cleaning of the root chamber–The root chamber must not be contaminated, or else diseases may strike the roots. So, you need to disinfect the root chamber every so often. Hydrogen peroxide is often used as disinfectant.

Higher cost–If you have technical competency, it isn't difficult to build your own system.

References

Alchimia. https://www.alchimiaweb.com/blogen/marijuana-growing-guide/nutrient-deficiencies-and-excesses-in-cannabis/

AmyL 2019 How to Grow Autoflowering Cannabis Plants. cprosolutions.com/uncategorized/how-to-grow-autoflowering-cannabis-plants/[1]

Bacci, L.; Battista, P.; Cardarelli, M.; Carmassi, G.; Rouphael, Y.; Incrocci, L.; Malorgio, F.; Pardossi, A.; Rapi, B.; Colla, G. Modelling Evapotranspiration of Container Crops for Irrigation Scheduling. In Evapotranspiration—From Measurements to Agricultural and Environmental Applications; Gerosa, G., Ed.; IntechOpen Limited: London, UK, 2011; pp. 263–282. ISBN 978-953-307-512-9.

Banks D. 2017. Mastering CO2: Ideal CO2 Levels for Growing Marijuana. https://www.maximumyield.com/mastering-co2-ideal-co2-levels-for-growing-marijuana/2/4073

Bell, K. 2016. https://medium.com/@kylephoenix/terpenes-are-the-aromatic-compounds-that-add-flavor-and-scents-to-your-cannabis-85ee679637d0

Berruti, A., Lumini, E., Balestrini, R.* and Bianciotto, V. Arbuscular Mycorrhizal Fungi as Natural Biofertilizers: Let's Benefit from Past Successes. 2016. https://www.frontiersin.org/articles/10.3389/fmicb.2015.01559/full

Biksa, E. 2017. Everything You Want to Know about Mother Plants and Clones.

https://hightimes.com/grow/everything-you-want-to-know-about-mother-plants-and-clones/

---

1. https://cprosolutions.com/uncategorized/how-to-grow-autoflowering-cannabis-plants/

Bond, C. 2017Bacteria? Virus? Fungi? Diagnosing Common Cannabis Diseases. https://www.maximumyield.com/bacteria-virus-fungi-diagnosing-common-cannabis-diseases/2/4950

Booth, J.K. & Bohlman, J. 2019. Terpenes in Cannabis sativa - From plant genome to humans.

Plant Science Volume 284, July 2019, Pages 67-72

Badertscher, K. and Badertscher, K. 2017. Grow Bigger Fatter Plants.

Brown, D. 2018. How to clean your drip irrigation filters. https://homeguides.sfgate.com/clean-drip-irrigation-filters-32594.html

Calculating Manure Application Rates. 2009. Manitoba Agriculture, Food and Rural Initiatives website: https://www.gov.mb.ca/agriculture/ environment/ nutrient-management/pubs/mmf_ calcmanureapprates _factsheet.pdf.

Cannabinoids. 2019 https://en.wikipedia.org/wiki/Cannabinoid

Caplan[2], D. M., Dixon, M. and Zheng, Y. 2017. Optimal Rate of Organic Fertilizer during the Flowering Stage for Cannabis Grown in Two Coir-based Substrates. Hortscience 52 (12) 12401-17.

Chandra, and El-Sohly, M. A. 2011. Photosynthetic response of Cannabis sativa L., an important medicinal plant, to elevated levels of CO2. Physiol Mol Biol Plants. 2011 Jul; 17(3): 291–295

Commercial Marijuana Hydroponic Systems. 2019. http://aquaponicsreviws.blogspot. com/2016/08/commercial-marijuana-hydroponic-systems.html.

---

2. https://www.researchgate.net/profile/

Deron_Caplan?_sg%5B0%5D=9BgLMVKWcyu8I6cEIngOkAf1V8Q76VYojojQFdQ0wvMS3yVqBXDs ECurbyFV7STbOZljKRc.Je33tqO58q39dVFjt4gkzpUhAFBviZoITDSbHUteTX340slGY9wO4sSPwo9-APgSUVA0Ofl5pOzvuQQOTMpFeA&_sg%5B1%5D=kQ2VZooF5i9-3FxdtOORng8lc5G0VFnnf0dMVv23TV8YN7XQStgKsv9atXj7ikS2NA2CoP7VvwHuzy2g.NfBvSYf7co QewXMaHoWGS1SzH60IJ8Gn7UM57EU8tKm5VW7oHFZ8G4p0auY5JG74TxMt8H5NSyeJNQNE w-Se4w

Courtney, A. 2018. Aeroponic Systems, Easy Guide to Growing with Aeroponics. https://smartgardenguide.com/aeroponics-systems-easy-guide/

Courtney, A. 2018. What are the advantages of Hydroponics? ttps://smartgardenguide.com/what-are-the-advantages-of-hydroponics/? unapproved= 876&moderation-hash=7288ebeac3a903602 da7f81e9122c98a#comment-876.

Currie, H.A. & Perry, C.P. 2007. Silica in Plants: Biological, Biochemical and Chemical Studies. Annals of Botany 100, 7: 1383–1389.

Deshmukh[3], R.K., Ma[4], J. F. and Bélanger[5], R. R

2017. Editorial: Role of Silicon in Plants. Plant Science. 25.

Ebb and Flow. 2019 Wikipedia. https://en.wikipedia.org/wiki/Ebb_and_flow

Fulcher, F.A.; Buxton, J.W.; Geneve, R.L. Developing a physiological-based, on-demand irrigation system for container production. Sci. Hortic. 2012, 138, 221–226.

Gershenzon, J. 2015. Changes in the Levels of Plant Secondary Metabolites Under Water and Nutrient Stress. In Recent Advances in Phytochemistry. Phytochemical Adaptations to Stress. 273-320.

History of Marijuana https://www.narconon.org /drug-information/ marijuana-history.html

How to clone Cannabis–Marijuana cuttings. 2019.https://cannabis-seeds-usa.org/clone-cannabis-marijuana-cuttings/

How To Germinate Autoflowering Marijuana Seeds. Growers Choice Cannabis Seeds. 2019.https://www.growerschoiceseeds.com/autoflowering-cannabis-seeds/how-to-germinate-autoflowering-marijuana-seeds/

How to use tensiometers? 2009.

3. http://www.frontiersin.org/people/u/103657

4. http://www.frontiersin.org/people/u/32294

5. http://www.frontiersin.org/people/u/194661

http://agriculture.vic.gov.au/agriculture/horticulture/vegetables/vegetable-growing-and-management/how-to-use-tensiometers

June-Wells, M. How Humidity Works

2017. https://www.cannabisbusinesstimes. com/article/moisture-matters/

Katan, J. 1980. Solar pasteurization of soils for disease control: status and prospects. Plant Disease 64: 45–54.

Katan, J. 1981. Solar heating (solarization) of soil for control of soil-borne pests. Annual. Review of Phytopathology, 19: 211–236.

Katan, J. 1987. Soil solarization, In: Innovative Approaches to Plant Disease Management, Chet, I., Ed., John Wiley & Sons, New York, p. 77.

Krueger, R. & McSorley, R. 2018. Nematode Management in Organic Agriculture http://edis.ifas.ufl.edu/ng047

Laing M. D., Gatarayiha M. C. and Adandonon A. 2006. Silicon Use For Pest Control In Agriculture: A Review. https://www.researchgate.net/publication/285063568_Silicon_use_for_pest_control_in_agriculture_A_review

Lipford, D. 2015. The Debate Over Organic Vs. Chemical Fertilizers. https://todayshomeowner.com/debate-over-organic-chemical-fertilizers/2/

List of Hemp Diseases. 2019. https://en.wikipedia.org/wiki/List_of_hemp_diseases

List of the Major Flavors & Fragrances Cannabis Produces. 2016 https://www.hytiva.com/ learn/discover-the-flavors-and-fragrances-of-cannabis

Manure. 2019. https://en.wikipedia.org/wiki/Manure

Mycorrhizal Inoculant. 2019. http://www.mykepro.com/mycorrhizae-benefits-application-and-research.aspx

McPartland, J.M. 1996. Cannabis Pests. http://www.internationalhempassociation.org/jiha/iha03201.html

Mushtaque M., G.M. Baloch and M.A. Ghani, 1973. Natural enemies of Papaver spp. and Cannabis sativa. Annual report, Commonwealth Institute of Biological Control, Pakistan station, pp. 54-5.

Nagy B., 1976. Host selection of the European corn borer (Ostrinia nubilalis Hbn.) populations in Hungary. Sym. Biol. Hung. 16:191-195.

Nagy B., 1986. European corn borer: historical background to the changes of the host plant pattern in the Carpathian basin. Proceedings of the 14th Symposium of the International Working Group on Ostrinia, pg. 174-181.

Neocleous, D., Katsoulas, N. and Kittas, C. Irrigation of Greenhouse Crops. 2019. file:///C:/AgroSearch/Cannabis%20Editing/horticulturae-05-00007-v2.pdf

Nutrient Film Technique (NFT) Hydroponic Systems. 2019. howtogrowmarijuana.com/nft-nutrient-film-technique/

Nuutinen, T. (2018): "Medicinal properties of terpenes found in Cannabis sativa and Humulus lupulus[6]". European Journal of Medicinal Chemistry, 157:198-228.

Opium as an international problem: the Geneva conferences–Westel Woodbury Willoughby[7] at Google Books[8]

Perveen, S. Introductory Chapter: Terpenes and Terpenoids. 2018. https://www.intechopen.com/

books/terpenes-and-terpenoids/introductory-chapter-terpenes-and-terpenoids

Potting Mixes. https://www.agric.wa.gov.au/ nursery-cut-flowers/potting-mixes

---

6. https://www.ncbi.nlm.nih.gov/pubmed/30096653

7. https://books.google.com/books?id=GJm-XDLJe1QC

8. https://en.wikipedia.org/wiki/Google_Books

Powdery   Mildew.   2018.   https://www.medicinalgenomics.com/powdery-mildew-2

Prior Stephen A. Prior² S.A., Runion²G.B., Marble, S.C., Rogers, H.H., Gilliam, C.H. and Torbert, H.A. 2011. A Review of Elevated Atmospheric CO_2 Effects on Plant Growth and Water Relations: Implications for Horticulture. HortScience46:2 pp 158-162.

Pyrethrins. 2015.

https://en.wikipedia.org/   wiki/Pyrethrinhttp://pmep.cce.cornell.edu/profiles/extoxnet/pyrethrins-ziram/pyrethrins-ext.html

Russo[9], E. 2007. "History of cannabis and its preparations in saga, science, and sobriquet". Chemistry & Biodiversity[10]. 4 (8): 1614–1648. doi[11]:10.1002/cbdv.200790144[12]

Ryz[13], N.R., Remillard[14], D. J. and Russo[15], E.B.2017. Cannabis Roots: A Traditional Therapy with Future Potential for Treating Inflammation and Pain. Cannabis Cannabinoid Res. 2017; 2(1): 210–216.

SARE   USDA.   Chemical   Characteristics   of   Manures.   2012. https://www.sare.org/Learning-Center/Books/Building-Soils-for-Better-Crops-3rd-Edition/Text-Version/Animal-Manures-for-Increasing-Organic-Matter-and-Supplying-Nutrients/Chemical-Characteristics-of-Manures

---

9. https://en.wikipedia.org/w/index.php?title=Ethan_Russo&action=edit&redlink=1

10. https://en.wikipedia.org/w/index.php?title=Chemistry_%26_Biodiversity&action=edit&redlink=1

11. https://en.wikipedia.org/wiki/Digital_object_identifier

12. https://doi.org/10.1002%2Fcbdv.200790144

13. https://www.ncbi.nlm.nih.gov/

    pubmed/?term=Ryz%20NR%5BAuthor%5D&cauthor=true&cauthor_uid=29082318

14. https://www.ncbi.nlm.nih.gov/

    pubmed/?term=Remillard%20DJ%5BAuthor%5D&cauthor=true&cauthor_uid=29082318

15. https://www.ncbi.nlm.nih.gov/

    pubmed/?term=Russo%20EB%5BAuthor%5D&cauthor=true&cauthor_uid=29082318

Shell meal https://www.7springsfarm.com/crustacean-meal-4-0-0-12-ca-w-high-levels-of-chitin-40-lb-bag/

Schnug, E., Jacobs, F., & Stoven, K. 2018. Guano: The White Gold of the Seabirds. https://www.intechopen.com/books/seabirds/guano-the-white-gold-of-the-seabirds

Sizing the Greenhouse Water System. 2019

https://ag.umass.edu/greenhouse-floriculture/fact-sheets/sizing-greenhouse-water-system

Smith, S. E., and Read, D. J. (2008). Mycorrhizal Symbiosis, 3rd Ed. London: Academic.

Soilless cultivation - What makes a good medium? 2019. http://www.canna-uk.com/ what makes good quality_soilless_growing_medium.

Somatic Mutation. 2019.

https://www.britannica.com/science/somatic-mutation

Staelens, S. 2017 "The Bhang Lassi Is How Hindus Drink Themselves High for Shiva"[16]. Vice.com. https://en.wikipedia.org/wiki/Bhang

Stafford; P. G., and Bigwood, J. (1992).

Psychedelics Encyclopedia[17]. Ronin Publishing.

The Scientific Principles of Crop Protection, by Hubert Martin. Fifth Edition. 1965. St. Martin's Press, New York. viii + 376 p.

The Opium and Narcotic Drug Act, 1923[18], S.C.[19] 1923, c. 22.

The Risk-Monger's Dirty Dozen—12 highly toxic pesticides approved for organic farming. 2016. https://risk-monger.com/2016/04/13/the-risk-

---

16. https://munchies.vice.com/en_us/article/kbx94a/httpmunchies-vice-comarticlesthe-bhang-lassi-is-how-hindus-drink-themselves-high-for-shiva

17. https://books.google.com/books?id=o4_pLqCOyDsC&pg=PA157

mongers-dirty-dozen-12-highly-toxic-pesticides-approved-for-use-in-organic-farming/

The Top Five Cannabis Diseases. 2019

https://www.blueskyorganics.com/growing-science/top-five-cannabis-diseases/

Thomas, M. 2012. Cannabis Cultivation: the complete Grower's Guide. https://www.academia.edu/30866208/ The_Only_Grow_Book_You_Will_Ever_Need_Green?auto=download

Understanding How Lumen Affect Plant Growth

https://www.lumigrowth.com/understanding-lumens/

Van Iersel, M., Burnett, S. and Kim, J. 2010.

How much water do your plants need?

https://www.greenhousemag.com/article/gmpro-0310-water-plants-automating-irrigation/

Vinje, E. Organic Fertilizers: What's all the fuss? 2017. https://www.planetnatural.com/big-stink/

Wang, K.-H., McSorley, R., Kokalis-Burelle, N. 2006. Effects of cover cropping, solarization, and soil fumigation on nematode communities. Plant and Soil 286: 229-243.

Wang, K.-H., McSorley, R., Marshall, A.J., Gallaher, R.N. 2004. Nematode community changes associated with decomposition of Crotalaria juncea amendment in litterbags. Applied Soil Ecology 27: 31-45.

---

18. https://archive.org/stream/
    actsofparl1923v01cana#page_6666cd76f96956469e7be39d750cc7d9_134_6666cd76f96956469e7be39d7
    50cc7d9_mode_6666cd76f96956469e7be39d750cc7d9_2up
19. https://en.wikipedia.org/wiki/Statutes_of_Canada

Weibelzahl-Fulton, E., Dickson, D.W., Whitty, E.B. 1996. Suppression of Meloidogyne incognita and M. javanica by Pasteuria penetrans in field soil, Journal of Nematology 28: 43-49. 1996.

Willoughby, W.W. (1925). "Opium as an international problem". Baltimore: The Johns Hopkins Press. Retrieved 2010-09-20.

Worms, B. 2019. Cannabis" viruses, a mysterious and devastating threat. https://www.dinafem.org/en/blog/cannabis-viruses-a-mysterious-devastating-threat/

www.ingramcontent.com/pod-product-compliance
Lightning Source LLC
Chambersburg PA
CBHW052043150726
48002CB00002B/728